DOUBLE-DIGIT GROWTH:

How to Achieve It with Services

Double-Digit Growth:
How to Achieve It with Services

Gunter PAULI

ESIF 3

Pauli Publishing

First edition 1991
© Gunter Pauli 1991

Pauli Publishing
't Hooghuys
B-2590 Berlaar
Belgium

A division of PPA Holding

ISBN 90-73625-02-5

Cover by Geert Plaisier
Printed in the European Community by De Rooster n.v. Belgium

To Carl-Olaf, of course.
He is my future.

If you love, love madly
If you threaten, threaten seriously
If you argue, argue bravely
If you punish,
you should have a reason,
When you forgive,
forgive with all your heart
When you celebrate,
celebrate till dawn.

Aleksey TOLSTOY
(1817 - 1875)

If you write, write with passion

(the author)

Acknowledgements

The task of researching and writing this book would have been vastly more difficult had it not been for the extraordinary assistance of Paul Luyten and Maurice Thys. Thanks are due also to Garsett Larosse for translating the manuscript into a book. An enormous debt of gratitude is owed to the many corporate managers and members of the European Service Industries Forum who gave so willingly of their time and shared data not available elsewhere. A special thanks to Eddie Crockett who rewrote my English into the language of a 20th century Shakespeare. Of course, not forgetting Karl Meersman, the very able cartoonist who interpreted several new and innovative services his way.

Table of Contents

Charts and Tables

Charts

Tables

Foreword

by Bessel Kok, CEO, S.W.I.F.T. sc

Gunter Pauli is a twentieth century crusader, a champion of the services industry cause. As an articulate advocate of the underestimated economic contribution of this sector. This has not been an altogether enviable task. Nevertheless - in the face of apathy, inertia and the malaise of disinterest - he has consistently and systematically hammered on doors in the corridors of influence to make people sit up, listen and act.

What he has to say is profoundly perceptive and of immense relevance to the future of employment and the future of our society. I have total admiration for people like Gunter Pauli, who never take no for an answer when seeking to advance the arguments in favour of an underrated element in the generation of national wealth. As the head of a service organization myself, I believe that we need more of Gunter's kind: more Don Quixotes to take up the gauntlet on behalf of our interests.

To many, service excellence is intangible, evident only in its absence. Some would argue that service can't be measured, that it's 'consumed' as it's delivered. However, it is manifest that poor service provokes a negative consumer reaction. Quality therefore needs to be both a principle and a process, not an afterthought at the end of the line - and, to be real, it must be measurable. Gunter Pauli vividly proves that it can, and should be.

I find it somewhat ironic that manufacturing industry has woken up to this truth, while many - perhaps most - in the services segment have not. In the context of escalating competitiveness, manufacturers realise that products form only a part of the market offer. They have instituted total quality strategies which focus priority on service issues. They have found the means to achieve this end: the core solutions which Gunter Pauli has been so ardently propounding in the dimension of the service industry for well over a decade.

This is more than a whimsical philosophy; it is a practical, pragmatic vision. Whatever he has to say deserves to be listened to closely. He cajoles attention. He prompts action. He is a man of boundless enthusiasm and infinite initiative. He commands my utter respect, and my wholehearted support.

If this books fails to shift the status quo and stand the attitudes of convention on their head, the service industry will be both the victim and the loser. We need urgent remedies, and Gunter Pauli is perhaps the best hope we have to catalyze the mandatory equation of change which will bring about sustained growth in services.

I therefore unreservedly commend this book. I also endorse Gunter Pauli for his persistence, dedication, confidence and complete, all-round competence.

Introduction

Progress is the result of initiatives taken by unreasonable men and women.

If I put one hand into freezing cold water and the other hand into boiling hot water, then - *on average* - I should feel no discomfort.

We all know that this is patently absurd.

Yet economists and accountants all too often resort to averages to explain, to decide, to evolve strategies. Key indicators such as GDP, inflation, unemployment, return on investment - all of these are averages which obscure the specifics of a given situation.

Averages make economists tick. And executives are all too often sidetracked by jargon and concepts which are divorced from day-to-day reality. But averages are simply irrelevant when it comes to identifying the most dynamic sectors of the world economy. Nor can jargon help us understand how their success can be sustained year-in, year-out.

Curiously enough, our politicians - and the media - consistently focus on the black spots in our economy. Few, if any, take the trouble to highlight success and growth - particularly double-digit growth.

This is what this book sets out to do.

This book is about growth, it is about what is best in our economy. And it is about the management style that makes it happen.

This book is not intended as a facile guide of the "How To..." variety. Instead, it prompts the reader to ask "Why not me, too?".

Compiling data, sifting evidence and collecting examples took over five years. Over 1,000 pages of facts, figures and case studies have been condensed into a slim volume which - one hopes - will be easily digested by those who are interested in Europe and its management style at their most successful.

The members of the European Service Industries Forum have given generously of their time and insight, none more so than ESIF President Bessel Kok, chief executive of S.W.I.F.T., whose patience, support, guidance and straight talking have provided an invaluable impetus.

This is my third book on services. The first two have sold over 100,000 copies in nine languages. These are certainly not my last words on the subject. Quite the contrary: I am only now beginning to appreciate the vast potential that services represent.

As it happens, today is my tenth anniversary as an entrepreneur. It was on May 7, 1981 that I set up my first company in Japan. A conference call between Tokyo, Antwerp and Dakar motivated three would-be entrepreneurs to take the plunge. Our start-up capital was a miserly ECU 5,000, but the barrier to entry was low and we willingly invested our time to make a success of our shared enterprise.

The business we started back then was certainly "unreasonable", but our youthful dynamism proved infectious. We survived the difficult early years, and have posted double-digit (35%) growth annually since 1985.

It is my own direct experience of services which has prompted me to write about them. If some of my enthusiasm rubs off on the reader, I shall feel more than rewarded.

Gunter Pauli
Between Paris and Brussels
May 7, 1991

CHAPTER ONE

Scenario 2016

SALZBURG, June 5, 2016. Today is Georges Posada's sixtieth birthday. The whole Posada family has arrived at Georges' splendid summer home on the Moon Lake just outside Salzburg. Celebrations are in full swing.

But the birthday boy simply cannot resist the temptation to steal away from the champagne, a delectable 1993 Bollinger Single Europe *cuvée*. He walks down the hall into his study to run a quick check on the latest updates on his 435 databanks and glance through the balance sheet printouts from his fourteen companies. And, while he is at it, Georges runs a computer simulation on his potential tax position to determine which of six different jurisdictions will be most advantageous.

Georges' daughter Astrid immediately guesses what her father is up to. She follows him into the study and peers over his shoulder, fascinated by the EuroTax Software Simulation Module. Astrid has just completed her dissertation at Budapest University - "ISDNs in Historical Perspective: A Diachronic Investigation". To Posada Senior goes at least some of the credit for her *summa cum laude*, because it was he who first fired her imagination. She could spend hours on end listening to his lurid tales of the bad old days, back when governments and hardware producers wasted whole decades fooling around with ludicrously complex norms and standards before finally getting their act together and welding telematics technologies into a basic but coherent global infrastructure. Georges Posada is still highly critical of the lack of insight of those erstwhile policymakers who had taken so interminably long to pinpoint the fundamental issue. As Georges never tires of repeating, "the mere availability of advanced technology does not make manufacturing industry and services more competitive. What we need is an internationally compatible infrastructure and people who know how to use it."

Georges' companies were among the first small enterprises to exploit the inefficiencies of one country to save on overheads in another. He had always found it incredible and infuriating how many outdated statutes kept blocking business expansion. It had not been until 1998 that small and medium-sized companies throughout Europe were allowed to lease and share a combined voice, image and data network. For decades, leased lines could only be used by the lessor who sent information along those lines for, at most, two or three hours a day. The lines were unused for the remaining twenty-one hours of the day - that was law.

It angered Georges every time he thought about it - the most profligate waste of resources in telecommunications history.

Finally, when thousands of small companies followed the example of the large transnationals and switched to London-based telex and fax networks, the continental telecommunications authorities got their just deserts: their business simply faded away. Suddenly, they had no option other than to institute crash programmes for long-overdue efficiency and cost-effectiveness. The protectionist option was thrown overboard.

Lydiastar, once a subsidiary of DHL, the company that had revolutionized business-to-business communications, had even received two Queen's Awards for Export Excellence for its success in luring away telecommunications customers from the continent to London.

As Astrid knew only too well, Georges Posada and his fellow entrepreneurs had their European strategy in place well before the magic date of December 31, 1992, when the European Community finally began to take shape as a genuinely "common" market. Georges and his colleagues had not simply waited around for it all to happen, lulling themselves into ever-deeper complacency. Not for them empty declarations along the lines of "We are ready for 1992" which many CEOs dutifully included in the foreword to the annual report.

No, indeed.

Georges had pushed hard to establish the first European service free trade zone in Zaventem, close to Brussels Airport. The Belgian government had realized that, if Brussels were really to develop as the service centre of Europe, then something drastic had to be done about its services infrastructure.

That was when it all started happening for Georges Posada.

The services zone at Brussels National was equipped with leading-edge telecommunications and information technology equipment. And telecommunication tariffs were held to a tenth of those elsewhere in Europe's capital. But that was not all. Every database anywhere in the world was accessible via one single access protocol - and at user rates which meant that they were consulted with unprecedented regularity.

The Zaventem Services Free Trade Zone was a runaway success. Communication-intensive service companies moved there in droves to set up shop: the world's leading courier firms, databases, teleshopping, telemarketing companies and computer telemaintenance enterprises. The auction house Christie's inaugurated the world's first teleauctioning network in Zaventem, using the high-quality cost-effective ISDN lines and satellite links which were provided as standard equipment in every single office unit.

Inevitably, success bred imitation. Convenient and low-cost access to global databases put Belgium squarely on the map as a good place to be. By 1990, there were already no fewer than 7,500 internationally accessible databanks available from Brussels and, by the turn of the century, this number had increased to 25,000.

These pioneering facilities for the design, development and commercial exploitation of dedicated databases worked like a dream. The success of the public network Minitel in France was infectious. As early as 1987, Germany had been obliged to buy into the 10,000 services offered on Minitel from France.

At long last, business had access to the information it so vitally needed.

Telemarketing became the name of the game throughout Europe. The idea had its roots in the United States and was subsequently adopted and developed in the United Kingdom before being exported to Continental Europe.

Not that it was all plain sailing. The need for multilingual telephone operators had posed an almost insurmountable barrier. And, of course, there were persistent obstacles in the form of out-of-date national legislation in several countries. All of this made telemarketing from Brussels a very attractive proposition.

According to Georges Posada's personal databank here on Moon Lake, the telemarketing industry now employed over 56,000 specialists who served Europe out of the Brussels Free Trade Zone. Germany, which had got off to an excellent start in the telemarketing stakes, lost out. Indeed, calling private German numbers from Germany to discuss sales or conduct market research was specifically outlawed. As a result, this telemarketing service was promptly offered from Brussels - in German, of course. The service was legally offered and sold in Belgium and, in accordance with the new principles of integrated European legislation, the service could no longer be proscribed in Germany. In practice, it would in any case have been a monumental monitoring task to check all international and digital telephone exchange traffic.

The Belgians had applied a basic rule: "Everything which is not regulated is permitted." In Germany, the rule had been different - "Everything which is permitted is regulated".

It was this shift in attitude and approach that finally imposed a radical change in the taxation systems throughout Europe. But, even although every European finance minister and every national tax authority had long recognized that the various systems were woefully inadequate, not one single country had made any fundamental change until after the turn of the century.

The taxation system of the 20th century had been designed in the early 19th century. Back then, it was customary to ask those in the top income brackets - less than 5% of the population - to declare their income. After all, paying taxes was a privilege. As far as tax revenues were concerned, these were guesstimated: no one had access to any concrete data. There were no bank accounts as we know them, no dividend payment tracking procedures, no transparent accounting systems, no financial disclosure rules. Oddly enough, governments kept on requiring tax returns in the same format for decades, even when all the pertinent information was electronically accessible and control systems were on hand within national boundaries.

One of the most successful software packages of the first years of the 21st century was EuroTax, which sold more than 100 million copies. Every European citizen with a computer had this software, a package that could be run on any machine and which stored every tax declaration form and fiscal system structure of the fifteen European Member States. Austria, Sweden and Norway had by this time joined the European Community, although Turkey was still on hold; in a national referendum in the late 1990s, the Swiss voted against EC accession.Even double digit inflation and a capital flight from Switzerland could not move the Swiss to opt for Europe.

EuroTax also featured a strategic tax planning feature which was indispensable to companies and individuals anxious to establish affiliate companies across Europe and spread their income across the continent. By that time, it had even become possible to allocate some income to Hungary, Bulgaria, Poland and the USSR. A series of new or renegotiated double taxation agreements master-minded by the European Commission and the International Fiscal Association now offered comprehensive protection against double taxation of income.

No middle or top-level executive now received his or her income in only his or her own country. The only revenue that scrupulously honest taxpayers declared in their home country was income from interest on foreign deposits. Here, too, the computer software proposed a series of possible alternative declarations and income spreads which took into account optimal corporate and individual allowances and deductions. Transnational corporations had been searching for the most fiscally advantageous route ever since they went global. But small companies had never had that possibility until the appropriate telecommunications system became available and the commensurate software was written.

EuroTax was set up and developed by four university graduates who felt so unhappy filing their first tax forms that they looked at it in a creative way.

As Georges Posada kept telling Astrid, creativity is often more important than experience.

Meanwhile, back at Moon Lake, Posada has run his tax planning programme. According to EuroTax, this particular *tranche* of income - ECU 87,000 - can best be allocated as follows: ECU 30,000 ECU in Belgium (where his daughter is now a postgraduate student at the UCL); this keeps Georges within the 20% fixed tax band without infringing his capital gains from stock options, which still enjoy tax-free status in Belgium. Next, EuroTax tells Georges to pay himself ECU 27,000 via his French subsidiary, ECU 15,000 through his Austrian company (which also owns and manages his databanks), and ECU 15,000 via an affiliate company in Sofia, Bulgaria (where his car lease contracts are registered).

By now, leasing has become truly international. National governments had long failed to understand or accept that vehicle fleet management companies will locate where statutory depreciation policies are most advantageous and where fiscal treatment of company cars is most lenient. If local tax treatment is punitive, then companies will move elsewhere.

The first country to lose out on the car leasing business was Belgium, followed by France and Germany. But the big surprise came when Bulgaria and Hungary decided to create special tax regimes for this kind of service via their financial operations in Vienna.

It was this kind of mobility coupled with low barriers to entry that Georges Posada had identified as the greatest single plus enjoyed by the services industry. Georges had done his homework, charting a course through the turbulent waters of European laws and regulations and identifying how and why whole service sectors relocated. To Georges' credit, he had warned several governments about the potential loss of revenue they faced, but all of them were too preoccupied by shorter-term issues such as budget deficits and felt they could not turn their attention to what, at the time, appeared to them to be a minor sector.

Belgium lost its car fleet management and leasing business, Germany lost its telemarketing, Denmark lost its teleshopping and mail-order companies.

Why?

Because, throughout Europe, the value-added tax rate of the country of origin was applied. With VAT on most consumer goods in Denmark running at 22% compared with, say, 14% in the Grand Duchy of Luxembourg, and with postage rates from Luxembourg 30% lower than in northern European Community member states, no right-thinking mail order and teleshopping company would stay long in Denmark.

Now, in 2016, Benetton has become the best-known insurance company in Europe. Benetton, the company that originally captured the imagination of European youth with its colourful shirts and sweaters before diversifying into insurance services. And 300 Belgian insurance companies which, for years, had protected their brokers in exchange for a comfortable commission did not know what had hit them. Integration of the European market for financial services was all well and good, they pointed out, but competition from a clothing and franchising group? What on earth was going on? Where did that idea spring from?

Before the Single Market was completed back in 1993, Georges Posada remembers how impressed various national policymakers had been with his argument that "1992" would help Japanese service companies and help them even more than their European counterparts.

Georges smiles to himself. Unfortunately, he had been right. By now, nobody raises an eyebrow when told that so-and-so banks with one of those foreign financial houses such as Dai Ichi Kangyo, Sumitomo or Fuji. Back then, it was all we could do to pronounce the names correctly. Today, of course, most people in international business speak fairly passable Japanese and Europeans no longer object to the Japanese presence and the scandals of the early 1990s are long forgotten. Of course, you have to hand it to the Japanese, they certainly know how to take care of their customers and .... they know how to spoil politicians as well. It's interesting how it all came about, thinks Georges. The Japanese learned their trade in California, then started purchasing every small bank they could lay their hands on and offering interest rates across the world which no one could match and few could refuse.

By the year 1995, twenty-two of the twenty-five largest banks in the world were Japanese, the largest of them being Nomura. Originally a securities house, Nomura succeeded in securing banking licences around the world long before they were ever permitted to undertake banking services in Japan. Only about ten years ago - in 2004 - they had made a successful bid for Citicorp's financial services division. It was strange how history repeated itself, thought Georges, recalling Sony's purchase in 1987 of the audio division of CBS as the prelude to Japan's takeover of Hollywood. And then we had Nomura securing control of Citibank to position themselves for a takeover of Wall Street a few years later. Some people had predicted this as early as 1985 when 10% of the New York Stock Exchange was already controlled by four Japanese brokers. And by now, noone remembers the scandals of insider trading on the Tokyo Stock Exchange. Still, who was to blame? Perhaps all those U.S. executives who opted for an armful of quick bucks?

Meanwhile, here in Europe, we now have a new breed of entrepreneurs spearheading the economic reconversion. The big names on the European business scene are no longer the North American transnationals in the oil or automotive business. On the contrary, the household names in Europe now are the networks of innovative, decentralized and fast-growing service companies - S.W.I.F.T., SGS, Adia, BET, ISS, Bertelsmann, Group 4 Securitas, ONCE, Club Med, Sodexho, Rentokil, ECCO, TMI, Minit International, Cap Gemini Sogeti, Randstad, Vedior, EF, Kwik-Fit, and so on.

Georges switches off his computer terminal, puts his arm around Astrid's shoulders and heads back toward the party.

It's strange, he thinks, what some of us realized decades ago still applies. There *are* no limits to the learning curve, there are no limits to human ingenuity and creativity. Manufacturing output increases are limited by raw materials, energy availability and access to capital, but services seem to have almost limitless potential. Not only are they environment-friendly, they are constrained only by the creativity of the individual.

All in all, Europe has found its niche in the world market for the provision of customized, high value-added, low-volume and human capital-intensive services. Unlike Japan, which resolutely went for high-volume, low value-added, price-sensitive and technology-driven services. Reuters was the first European brand name to go under in this service sector - merged with Quick of Japan.

The U.S. service industry never did seem able to make up its mind. Even now, in 2016, with 91% of the American population employed in the services sector, they are still mainly servicing their domestic market.

Will Europe succeed? A lot will depend on the strategies that leading European services companies apply in order to innovate and to identify the whole of Europe as a natural domestic market. And a lot will depend on how successful they are in establishing a network of related companies with an excellent information gathering and distribution system that permits them to monitor continuously market threats and market opportunities.

"Welcome back, Georges. What on earth have you been doing all this time?" Martha Posada hands Georges a slender *flûte* of champagne.

"Excuse me, I was checking on a couple of items. Having a chat with Astrid, as it happens. You know, I was just saying to her that the European Commission and several of the Member State governments really *must* get to grips with the dynamics of the services sector. After all, that's where you get double digit growth which is not attributable to lower energy prices or interest rate subsidies."

"Georges, it's June 5, 2016. It's your birthday, remember? What do you think: should we put the world's problems aside for a few hours and focus on dinner?"

"Martha, you are absolutely right, as usual. But it's a fascinating subject, after all. Astrid was just saying..."

"Georges - dinner!"

We wish Georges, Martha, Astrid and their guests a pleasant evening and leave them to their own devices.

Let's take up the discussion where Astrid and Georges left off.

Let's take a more detailed look at how Europe is performing *today* in a market sector where demand is of the double-digit variety.

If Georges turns out to have been right, and if present trends are anything to go by, then Europe indeed has a bright future. For that future to materialize, however, we need policies, a business environment and a management style which are services friendly.

Let us hope that those policies, that environment and that management style can be put in place and remain there. And that the management and the entrepreneurs are around to make it happen.

CHAPTER TWO

Question Time

This book attempts to answer a series of interrelated questions which have surfaced time and again in discussions between the author and public and private enterprises worldwide:

* **Why** have services consistently outperformed manufacturing over recent decades?
* **Why** have specific services sectors consistently posted double-digit growth?
* **Why** have individual services companies succeeded where others have failed?
* **Why** do the world's leading services companies internationalize more effectively than their manufacturing industry counterparts?
* **What** are the salient features of a successful services organization?
* **What** are the key issues which services companies must address if they are to achieve and sustain double-digit growth?
* **What** can manufacturing industry learn from the services sector?
* **What** are the prospects of manufacturing industry and the services sector twinning for growth?
* **How** can lessons learned in the services sector be transposed to its public sector counterpart?
* **How** must management adapt to the specifics of services?
* **How** can today's services develop a corporate culture which will ensure continued double-digit growth?
* **How** serious is the Japanese challenge in the services sector?

These and related issues are explored on the basis of case-by-case analysis of market leaders in the services sector: companies which have demonstrated that year-on-year double-digit growth is no longer a myth but a reality.

CHAPTER THREE

Services and the Magic of Double-Digit Growth

That large parts of Europe - diagnosed not so very long ago as a victim of Eurosclerosis - could today be enjoying double-digit growth rates seems absurd. After all, double-digit growth rates are not characteristic of the developed world. They appear only occasionally, erupting as some underdeveloped nation rushes to catch up with the industrialized West: Japan in the 1960s, South Korea in the early 1980s. After South Korea, Taiwan and Thailand have also been double-digit growers.

The International Monetary Fund's most recent **World Economic Outlook** confirms that double-digit growth is not a characteristic feature of the developed world. Apart from Japan, with 3.7% year-on-year GNP growth, no other major OECD country recorded a growth rate above 3% in 1990.

However, the OECD figures are averages which obscure the most dynamic sectors. Sadly, too little information is available on the sunrise sectors of our economies - most of them in services industries.

The European Services Industry Forum (ESIF) has repeatedly argued for detailed statistics. Action has begun, but it will be another four to five years before genuinely comparable data become available. In the meantime, it is still a major task to detect those parts of Europe's economy that are enjoying double-digit growth.

That said, ESIF has succeeded in pinpointing some fifty double-digit growth service sectors based on an analysis of fast-growing service companies across Europe. And it is time to ask a couple of basic questions.

Why are these companies' markets growing so fast?

And how are Europe's most successful service companies coping with this tremendous growth?

Why are Services Growing at Double-Digit Rates?

Spectacular growth is not simply the result of a sudden upsurge in our appetite for services. The growth in demand is mainly the result of a tremendous need for improved efficiency. It is the result of a considered response by both established companies and new entrepreneurs.

New services are like music. It is pointless to ask someone who has never listened to music if he or she prefers Vivaldi to Mozart or Mahler. Similarly, if you have never consulted a database or if you have never had the opportunity to try out telebanking on a Sunday morning from your bedroom, it will be difficult for you to comprehend how MINITEL in France keeps on growing at explosive rates. There are two reasons why the market for new services is growing so fast - regardless of government intervention and notwithstanding the restrictive policies that still prevail.

The *first* reason is that the service infrastructure of computers, telecommunications and home electronics creates opportunities. A host of potential new services are unleashed with the introduction of digital communications, mobile communications, VANs and LANs. An additional boost can be expected from the full-scale introduction of integrated services digital networks in the 1990s.

It suffices to note the various new terms that have found their way into our daily vocabulary: teleshopping, telemarketing, teleconferencing, teleprinting, telebanking, telecontrol, even telebetting and teleauctioning. Library services used to be in one place, inaccessible after working hours. By contrast, a databank transcends national and physical boundaries - at any given time.

The world market for database services was assessed in 1990 at ECU 9 billion, up an astonishing ECU 5 billion on 1985. The more modems that find their way into the services infrastructure, the longer double-digit growth in this sector will be maintained.

Today, Maxwell Online, the databank network of the Maxwell Communications group, integrates over 250 databases which may be accessed from virtually anywhere in the world.

The *second* reason why several new services are booming is because they are becoming more professional - being transformed from "spare bedroom" operations into fully-fledged organizational technologies. This is not only true for high-tech services, which comprise a wide range of computer and communications networks, but also for basic down-to-earth services. Why is my cleaning lady at home not as efficient and productive as the outside firm that cleans my office? How come a catering firm seems to do even better than my excellent cook?

The recourse to out-of-house services, also called externalization, de-integration, out-sourcing, or out-contracting, is the result of a leapfrogging in productivity and efficiency - of a professionalization which makes it impossible to continue with in-house suppliers of the service.

We have become accustomed to believing that industry can "industrialize", "standardize", and "boost productivity". But we still tend to consider services as a local activity where breakthroughs cannot be achieved because the major input is people.

This is a fallacy.

Successful service companies have clearly understood their markets, charted the flow of their services and perfected each single step.

Preparing a hamburger is not a high-tech job. Yet there is only one company in the world which succeeds in preparing and selling four billion hamburgers every year. Even a small part of the hamburger "package" - the French fries, - has been perfected to the level of the genetically engineered McDonald potato and the timing of each move of the deep-frying process.

Accordingly, it would be wrong to claim that the growth in services is mainly due to their externalization by industry. Of course, industry **is** externalizing its services. After many years of searching for more productivity in the production process, industry has come to realize that it also has to improve efficiency in the other 75% of the value added that it processes: in other words, in services to production. This not only involves complete externalization i.e. the discontinuation of a service previously procured in-house, it also involves the transformation of an inefficient in-house service or outside-procured one into a highly competitive internal one which is then used in-house but also offered out-of-house on the market. In that sense it becomes "internalized".

To cite concrete examples, advertising, cleaning and security services are

---

How big is the market?

Since 1987, the author has attempted to estimate world turnover for fifty new services in ECU billions. The lack of exact data precludes precise figures. That said, information made available to the author by the market leaders allows the order of magnitude to be assessed with some degree of accuracy. The figures in this study have to be interpreted as best estimates. Markets cannot yet be segmented in such a way as to make possible a clear identification of market trends. There is a need to evolve like in manufacturing: we no longer talk about "textiles", but break the industry down according to specific products (carpets, clothing, upholstery fabrics) or grade (cotton, pure wool, acrylic), or fabrication method (airjet, jacquard). We are obliged to proceed in the same way for services if we are to identify the dynamics and the market shifts per sector.

One thing is clear, however. Demand for these services is growing and, estimates apart, it is clear that each is a double-digit growth market.

As might be expected, the rate of growth is not double-digit every single year and not the same in every country. A few sectors that had previously been booming in one country are experiencing a slowdown and even negative growth rates in another. This book looks at European trends, unless otherwise indicated.

---

typically contracted out. But, in large companies, maintenance services, warehousing, training, and financial services are increasingly handled in-house and offered to the market at competitive prices.

Caterpillar, for example, has developed one of the largest fast-response parts systems in an effort to supply clients with their spares. Caterpillar has sold 20,000 of its mechanical shovels worldwide, and can meet 98% of requests for spare parts from its 100,000-part inventory in less than 24 hours. Once the company had solved its own network problems, it set up Caterpillar Logistics and Distribution Systems to provide logistics and fast transportation services to other large manufacturers.

In April 1991, Caterpillar Logistics landed its biggest and most comprehensive contract so far, agreeing with Chrysler to handle pan-European distribution of replacement parts. Revenues from this "third-party distribution activity" have been rising by 30% a year.

Why are Some Service Companies More Competitive?

Markets are expanding fast, but this does not explain why market leaders become leaders and remain so.

Why is ISS of Denmark able to clean a building or Group 4 Securitas make a building secure so much better than many of their respective competitors?

Any successful service can and will attract many imitators. What is crucial in order to develop a competitive edge is to understand how such an edge is built up.

Conventional economic theory has it that the competitive edge of a company derives from the efficient combination of four inputs: raw materials, capital, labour and technology. Lower coal and iron-ore prices, lower interest rates, better educated personnel, and access to state-of-the-art technology would make an industrial group hard to beat.

Service companies, of course, have no such raw material problems. The capital needed to start a service company is marginal compared with that required to set up a factory. Moreover, technology has not (yet) swept all before it: in services companies, people are *the* key factor.

In the evening, the capital of a services company walks out through the front door - and the owner hopes that it will come back next morning. People are what gives a competitive edge to a services company. But they must be people who *understand* the service concept and are committed to perfecting each single step in the process of delivering consumer satisfaction.

Here, we are not simply talking about the mere application of "management techniques", we are referring to the development of "an organizational technology" for the specific service in question.

This organizational technology manifests itself in the marketplace in two forms: first, as a rapid increase in productivity and, second, as improved flexibility in adapting to consumer needs. It is this fast increase in productivity which has led to the capacity to sweep a building clean at the rate of 400 square metres an hour. This has made it possible to shorten the time between pick-up and delivery of an urgent envelope through a courier service by no less than two hours each year. Equally, it is improved flexibility which means that a client can keep track of each envelope he has mailed through a system that tracks each of seven intermediate steps through which the delivery is routed.

In short, the service of selling time has been complemented by services which offer greater reliability and security - a clear response to marketplace demand. The competitive edge of a company is determined in the first instance by its organizational technology and, in the second place, by its ability to use computers, telecommunications and electronics better than its competitors. The key issue is not whether to invest in computer and communications networks, but how best to utilize the infrastructure that is readily available for the process of defining, analyzing and offering a specific service.

How Do Services Companies Cope with Double-Digit Growth?

How can services companies consistently cope with growing demand while remaining highly competitive?

In the case of the newest services - where there is scarcely any pre-existing market structure and where barriers to entry are very low, fresh start-ups emerge overnight. Human resources are mobilized through teamwork, where the major investment is in time and where the joy of launching a business is central.

Start-up capital can come in the form of a contract with the first client, and the service infrastructure of the company can be dependent on the public network. This process is easy. And doubling annual revenue from, say, ECU 20,000 to ECU 40,000 is not too difficult.

But a new services company can fall into a major marketing trap. It is impossible for it to undertake full-scale market research as manufacturing industry does. A prototype of the service cannot be tested locally. Services are intangible. As a consequence, new service companies have to sell their ideas to a small group of potential clients who have faith and trust in those people who are offering the service. In so doing, they thus create a captive market which shepherds them through the process of moving their concept from the "spare bedroom" through to the professional level.

Service companies never seem to have encountered difficulties in finding money to get started, or finding cash to grow further. Private placements have been most successful. Only the stock exchanges have been reluctant to finance service companies. It is therefore no surprise that most of the leading service companies are still privately held and that growth is financed more on the basis of retained profits than on third party financing. The reward for the initial investors has been more in terms of capital gains than a mere dividend pay-out.

The software market, for example, is characterized by such an entrepreneural atmosphere. The EC software market for 1991 is estimated at ECU 32 billion. Last year, it was valued at 29 billion ECU. Only a handful of software companies are quoted on the stock exchange, Cap Gemini Sogeti perhaps being a large exception. Yet at least half of the 800 software companies operating in Belgium today will go out of business in the course of the next three years.

Unfortunately, no one can accurately predict which half.

This being the case, it is instructive - not to say imperative - to examine how successful companies navigate in this double-digit growth environment and how they succeed in sustaining such growth for ten to twenty years at a stretch.

Going International: Replication

Once a company has developed a genuine understanding for the services it provides and has acquired a leading organizational technology, its next step will be to aim for organizational economies of scale. In other words, it will look to replicate its existing, perfectly functioning operation somewhere else.

Consider the explosive growth of Minit International, the world leader for shoe repair and key copying, with 4,700 outlets worldwide, 11,000 employees and a turnover of half a billion ECU; or that of Kwik-Fit, the largest independent car tyre and exhaust replacement company in Europe operating out of over 600 individual centres, having 3,500 employees and a ECU 329 million turnover. Each designed an organizational technology for a simple service which they then replicated hundreds of times. Of course, their success has attracted imitators, but no one so far has matched their level of sophistication - although "anybody" can fit a new exhaust or make a duplicate key. Meantime, both companies maintain double-digit growth rates.

Strategies for Diversification

To keep a competitive edge and maintain double-digit growth over a long period of time, organizational economies of scale alone will not be sufficient. A second step is needed: diversification.

Diversification is easier said than done. Because an entrepreneur has mastered an organizational technology in one service does not necessarily imply that he can do so in another. The reverse is more often the case. This is because, each time around, there is a fresh need to understand the specific process of each specific service, however close it may appear to be to the services sector in which the company has already acquired a competitive edge.

To put it bluntly, there is no such thing as a "generally applicable service management technique".

Arguably, there are *four* possible strategies for diversification.

Table 3-1. Diversification Strategies

1. Launch new activities in closely related services
2. Optimize your services' infrastructure
3. Offer training
4. Move from services into production

Source: author, 1987

The *first* is to launch new activities in closely related services. Careful study of each market segment will bring to light a set of potential complementary services. These will emerge as clusters of related services. Each leading company in its own sector will enjoy a low entry barrier to the other sector. If it succeeds in developing an organizational technology in the related market, then its growth strategy will be synergistic.

Table 3-2. Example of clusters in complementary services

Language services Training Software Electronic publishing Marketing and communication	Cleaning and maintenance Refurbishing Security services Linen washing Temporary employment
Courier services High quality fax Remailing Telex networks Parcels	Disaster recovery Computer maintenance Facilities management Custom designed software Network design Electronic archiving

Source: author

Language services offer a clear example. The world market for language services was estimated in 1990 at ECU 18 billion, up 40% on 1987. Japan alone is responsible for approximately ECU 8 billion. *If* you are in language services and have developed full electronic mail capability, *if* you are able to cope with fifteen different languages, *if* you have built up your specialized language "tool boxes" (or language databanks), *if* you have designed your specialist software support, *if* you have a network of translators each working back into his or her mother tongue, and *if* you have acquired specialist expertise over a range of market segments such as automotive, pharmaceuticals or electronics, *then* you are poised for diversification into further sectors.

There is one proviso, of course: that your core business of language service has evolved from a spare bedroom service into a genuine organizational technology. Once they have internationalized through organizational economies of scale, language service companies move into electronic publishing, language training and software. By the same token, software companies that have to cope with translations all the time and publishers who go international are all moving into one another's fields.

The corporate strategist will readily appreciate how complex it is to effect a competitive analysis in circumstances where the competition can come literally, from *anywhere*...

The *second* type of diversification is inspired by the need to optimize the service infrastructure. Once an electronic distribution channel is installed, a company is clearly well advised to investigate the possibility of offering its clients new services through the same computer and communications line. The parallel here is the production manager with a new production unit for which he has only one 8-hour shift of work: he will want to line up subcontracts which bring the level of utilization of his equipment up to twenty-four hours a day. Equally, since computers and telecommunications often represent the second-largest capital cost for most new services, those companies will try to integrate additional business by way of their electronic distribution channel.

Additional services have two purposes: first, to optimize returns on investment in computer and telecommunications and, second, to increase consumer loyalty by offering additional services free or at low price. Hertz rental cars offers a multilingual guide to help the traveller to find hotels, government services, conference and sports facilities in every large city in the United States. That helps to create customer loyalty.

In Europe, investment on computer and telecom systems runs up to ECU 5,000 per employee per year in the financial sector. In Britain, Citicorp spends nearly ECU 40,000 on information technology per account executive every three years. When a bank has invested heavily in EFTPOS (electronic fund transfer at point of sale), why should it not offer other services on its network? And when a retailer invests in EFTPOS, is it not obvious that each is trying to invade the other's traditionally distinct services?

Marks and Spencer of the United Kingdom runs its own credit card on the market; EFTPOS operations can be performed with the card. Is Marks and Spencer in retailing or in financial services?

Once the likes of DHL, TNT Express Worldwide and Fedex have established car fleets around the country to pick up and deliver parcels and documents, a stable of cargo planes and a sophisticated telecommunications and computer network which allows them to track all shipments entrusted to them, it is self-evident that they can offer more than just fast and personalized mail. Using the same distribution channels, they can diversify into other services without incurring major add-on costs.

DHL, for example, offers a high-quality fax and telex network. And all the major courier service companies offer remailing facilities. These companies remain in their area of specialization but they offer additional services which use upgraded distribution channels to the fullest extent, and which respond to a real market demand.

Cap Gemini Sogeti entered the market for custom designed software in 1974. Having carved out a market leadership in software, Cap Gemini Sogeti diversified into computer services which include systems integration, facilities management and consulting. Cap Gemini Sogeti recognizes that the world market for professional IT related services generates more turnover in "other services" combined than in the customized software.

Chart 3-1. Worldwide Information & Telecommunication Professional Services Market

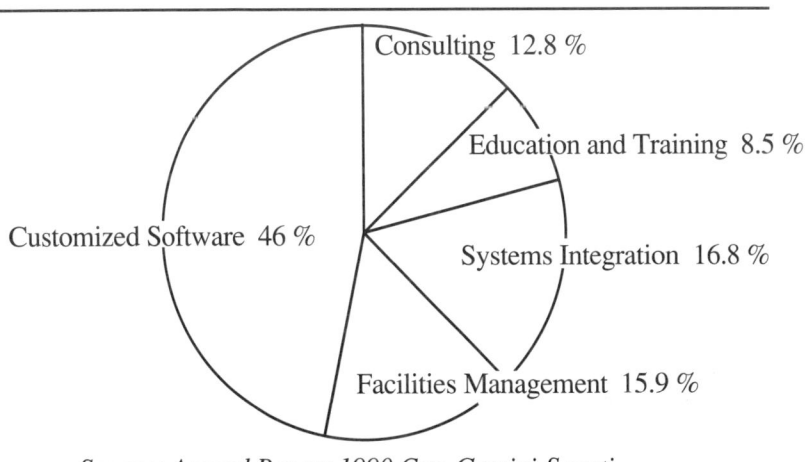

Source: Annual Report 1990 Cap-Gemini-Sogeti

A *third* strategy for diversification is to offer training.

In information technology and telecommunications, nearly 10% of turnover is in education and training. If you are the leading customized software specialist, you can train your clients better than anyone else.

Everyone senses the need filled by new services, but few really understand what they are all about. This presents an ideal opportunity for training. Although rarely foreseen in business plans, the training of clients and would-be clients often turns out to generate 10-20 % of turnover and grows at double-digit rates along with the rest of the business. After all, if you succeed in becoming a market leader in telemarketing, for example, then you are ideally placed to offer training to every switchboard operator in the Top 500.

The *fourth* strategy for diversification is to move into manufacturing of certain products. Even though this may seem a very bold step, it is a logical evolution in several market sectors. Indeed, service companies are now playing a key role in the development of new applied technologies. Few computer and telecom conglomerates consider the market for new services of sufficient volume to tailor some of their products to those market needs. As a result, service companies themselves invest heavily in informatics systems which permit them to tailor the infrastructure to their organization.

Two leading security service companies in Europe, Group 4 Securitas and Randstad, have diversified into the engineering and production of electronic alarm equipment. Telindus, originally only a distributor and designer of modems, has decided to manufacture customized modems. And, from there, it offered integrated communication systems design, installation and maintenance. Not surprisingly, Tel*indus* has now changed its name to Tel*info*.

In practice, the large majority of diversification projects are decentralized, which is to say that they are performed by independent units which exhibit a small degree of synergy with the other services offered by the company in question. This is important. No service can be considered as an annex to another. If each service is to develop into a genuine organizational technology, then it has to be considered and structured as an independent profit centre. In this way, services conglomerates can emerge as genuine business support service providers.

The financing of diversification brings with it several bottlenecks. To some extent, new and expanded contracts with clients may provide a sound financial base. But barriers to entry are low. As a result, it is noticeable that successful companies often invite their largest clients to become shareholders. This "captive-market strategy" offers a much-needed breathing space during which the new service can be translated into a well-adapted organizational technology in its own right.

Specialization Strategies

Diversification is not the panacea for growth. Several service companies have learned this the hard way. Recently, the two market leaders in quality control and inspection services, SGS and Inspectorate, entered into bold diversification strategies. While SGS ventured along the careful route, Inspectorate engineered a merger with ADIA, the world's number two in temporary employment. It took a mere two years until the new shareholders noticed that there was "no logic in the logic". And ADIA is going back to its core business.

This is a learning process and the pendulum will move from left to right, from one extreme to the other till the management finds the right mixture of services. After all, it is not the purpose to offer *any*thing *any*time to *any* client who asks for it.

Growth can be measured in two ways: increase of turnover, or increase of value added generated by the company. Specialization is very often the way to generate more margin for the company by adapting to the needs and requirements of hundreds of sub-segments of the market.

Cleaning services have opted over the past decade for diversification, as have temporary employment and security services. Now, the market leaders have a portfolio of services on hand and pursue an overall specialization route. En route, some of the activities may be sold, some may be expanded. A highly dynamic process is set in motion. ISS has sold its security operations in the Netherlands, but is now active in hospital cleaning and food hygiene, snapping up the contract to sweep the Carlsberg beer factory clean.

The cleaning of an office building, a school, a hospital, computer keyboards, a food processing factory, the Royal Palace, the Museum of Modern Art does require a specialist approach. You cannot compare the sweeping of a dust free room with the cleaning of an entrance hall of a ministry. A security company must specialize and develop its organizational technologies per client. Are we talking about the manned guarding of a museum, the security of an electronic network, the transport of valuables, the storage of security archives, electronic monitoring of entrance and exit, or an alarm centre connecting 1,000 sensors or is the company anxious to undertake a mere safety audit?

When the margin for the cleaning of an office building can be as low as 4% of the contract, then growth in volume must prepare the way for growth in margins. Specialization is the only opportunity because, as will be explained in the last chapter, economies of scale and economies of scope both have their limits in the market for new and innovative services.

Human Resource Management

Internationalization, diversification and specialization along specific lines are three underlying strategies for double-digit growth. The key element, however, remains human resource management.

How is this accomplished effectively? How can a young firm cope with another new employee every day? How can it integrate 10,000 new employees in a year in the wake of a series of acquisitions around the globe?

Situations such as these can lead to chaos. There is, however, no real reason why chaos should lead to bankruptcy. Services are most successful in a "self-organizing universe".(*)

The first thing to note in the case of major service sector firms is the virtual non-existence of headquarters. A whole series of double-digit growth companies with some ECU 1 billion-plus in annual turnover seem to manage with a head office of less than 100 people - including secretarial and other support staff.

Fast-growing service companies do not seem to need forty-storey buildings where all operations are centralized. Vendex International, one of the largest multi-service companies in the world - with an estimated ECU 8 billion turnover in 1990 - has only 41 people in its central office. DHL International, which coordinates operations in 186 countries, has only 140 people in its head office. Such a lightweight superstructure is only feasible under four conditions:

* Processing the service is highly professionalized
* Decision-making is decentralized, fast and effective
* The company has a strong corporate culture; and
* Each employee understands his or her role in the overall framework and contributes drive, commitment and imagination.

Dynamic service companies do not simply grow, they also *train*. Although fast growth does not permit staff to be trained years or even months before they become operational, there is always the practicality of on-the-job training. Typically, the workforce will indicate to management the areas where they wish to have further training. Interestingly, it does seem to be the employee who first identifies his lack of specific skills, following which the human resources manager sets about organizing the necessary training facilities.

In a "top-light" management structure, employees tend to make life easy for their superiors. Instead of bombarding higher-up colleagues with requests for solutions to problems, they turn into problem-solvers themselves. This is a fundamental characteristic of fast-growing services companies with a small central

---

* *Erich Jantsch wrote a book "The self-organizing universe"*

office. It suffices to ask how the headquarters of DHL International could cope if all 186 countries around the world were to rely on Brussels to find an answer to each individual problem that arises.

Training is the key.

Training not only contributes to corporate culture, it also enhances basic skills and social values at the level of the workforce. And these skills and values are badly needed in the fast internationalization, diversification and specialization process that new services companies undergo.

Overall, flexibility, social values and language skills emerge as the three main attributes of employees in double-digit growth service companies.

Flexibility is vital to cope with the changing needs of the market, which the employees often have to sense themselves.

As operations are decentralized and spread globally, quality control emerges as an additional key component in services. When you sell a malfunctioning radio, you can replace the radio. When you waste your client's time by rendering bad service, you can refund the client's cash but you cannot give back the lost time. The streamlined headquarters of service companies do not admit centralized management. This is a crucial part of the professionalization of services. Each employee knows clearly which standards to take into consideration. Those who do not know have to learn on-the-job and have to learn quickly. There is no time to waste in a growth environment. There is no place for waste in the services sector.

Given that the antennae of the market are so important, their motivation is central. Services companies depend on people, so their double-digit growth is tenuous or secure depending on whether their employees identify with the firm's objectives and are motivated to attain them.

A discussion of fiscal policies is perhaps out of place in the present context. But the time has come when governments *must* stop taxing on the basis of an industrial economy. Entrepreneurs who invest their time and generate a multitude of value added for the economy should be rewarded for their long-term approach. Stock option programmes for all employees and tax-free capital gains should be streamlined across Europe to motivate all stake-holders to opt for long-term growth. Europe has to avoid at all cost that dividend pay-out is taxed less than capital gains. If dividends enjoy lower taxation rates, then the system is based on the principle that the government and the shareholders know better what to do with the cash generated by the enterprise than its management, employees and entrepreneurs!

Government regulation has not succeeded in blocking services companies from satisfying growing demand. Outdated telecom policies do create inconvenience, but the great advantage of services is that they are "invisible". So, if too many problems are imposed, the service will still be performed - but in the black or parallel economy. Or the service will simply be offered from another country.

Summing Up

There is not one business school anywhere in the world that teaches its students how to manage the chaos inherent in double-digit growth services companies. And, to be fair, there is no commonly applicable recipe for all services.

Every sector which is new benefits from double digit-growth, but never in recent economic history have we paid so much attention to technology and smoke stack industries, whereas over fifty sectors which are booming at double-digit rates are hardly noticed.

Even though double-digit growth is still the exception rather than the rule, the economic reconversion of Europe will depend more on these new fast-growing sectors where the vast majority of new jobs are created than on the better-documented sectors which look likely to be characterized by low growth for years to come. After all, manufacturing industry needs services badly if it is to leapfrog.

Europe must realize that it has a potentially enormous advantage in a number of services areas. If economic policymakers - i.e., the representatives of the private sector, government and labour unions - take the trouble to understand how those services companies operate, why they are competitive and how they may remain so, and in what a fragile environment they navigate, then the countries of Europe will be better-placed to design together a service-friendly policy environment. But policy makers are still too limited in their approach, largely because they only think and operate in a manufacturing industry mode.

At a time when the added value generated by manufacturing is well over 75 % determined by services, the role of the services sector is not only a matter of intellectual curiosity, it is a matter of survival in the midst of fierce competition where production of goods meets a buyers' market.

Industry needs services. So much is obvious when looking at the bottom line. Accordingly, before we go on to highlight fundamental differences between manufacturing and services, let's take a broad look at how services are booming and how manufacturing industry and services can twin for growth.

CHAPTER FOUR

Manufacturing and Services: Twinning for Growth

Many manufacturing companies have discovered that they can handle their accounting, legal services, payroll, maintenance, repair, personnel administration, research and design much more efficiently out-of-house than in-house. McKinsey suggests that the actual implementation in a number of non-core tasks is better done by outsiders who will do the job at less than half the cost, in one-third of the time and using one-fifth the number of people than for any in-house solution (case from the IT services).

This externalization has undoubtedly contributed to the rapid growth of business services. As 75% of the value added created in manufacturing derives from services to production, there is tremendous scope for improvements in speed, efficiency and effectiveness in manufacturing.

In a nutshell, manufacturers seeking competitive advantages in today's world cannot separate manufacturing operations and service technologies.

In the European Community, the business services sector today accounts for about 6% of Community GNP and represents about 14 % of the value added of all market services. With the markets expanding at the rate of some 15 % per year, business services are growing rapidly, with the highest growth rate in the tertiary market sector. In the EC, business services represent 5.5 million jobs and the business services sector boasted a turnover of ECU 250 billion in 1990.

Manufacturing industry boosts the services sector by externalizing services. But industry also extends its scope of activities by taking over service functions:

*   The drive for quality in home appliances and cars has decreased both the time and the cost of maintenance and repair. Whereas cars needed servicing after 3,000 kilometres only ten years ago, some only need maintenance after 15,000 kilometres today.
*   Prepared gourmet foods, convenience mixes and microwave dinners have been substituted for restaurant services.
*   Video films, rented at the video shop on the corner, have substituted for the service offered by the movie theatre.

These examples suffice to demonstrate that industry's integration and externalization of services have a double-edged effect on GNP and employment in the tertiary sector.

Mr Charles "Chuck" Exley, head of NCR, has been nominated several times by **Fortune** as America's most valued manager. Exley has launched a programme which offers nineteen different services to its product and systems range. One NCR marketing executive notes that, by the turn of the century, as much as 80% of profits may very well come from those services.

Table 4-1. Evolution of IBM turnover 1980-1990 (%)

	1980	1990
Maintenance	11	8
Services	16	24
Software	6	17
Hardware	67	51
	100%	100%

Source: IBM, Paris 1991

IBM has noted - to no-one's surprise - that the share of pure services (excluding software and maintenance) in its total turnover increased from 16% in 1980 to 24% in 1990. Thanks to improved quality, maintenance lost 3% out of total sales whereas software jumped from 6 to 17% over one decade. In 1991, IBM generated for the first time more revenues from services than from hardware sales. And, if we consider profit, services represent already 60% of the bottom line. Services will soon be soon at the core of IBM's financial success - or should we say survival?

Hewlett-Packard reports that, in 1990, growth in services had for the first time overtaken growth in products. Whereas equipment sales only increased by 8%, services maintained a healthy 21% growth, up from 17% one year earlier. One of the main reasons for the lower growth in hardware sales is that Hewlett-Packard has to give larger discounts to volume purchasers such as dealers and OEMs.

The diversification of industry into services is exemplified by the establishment of 150 new branches of First Nationwide Bank, the fast-growing savings and loan subsidiary of the Ford Motor Company, at branches of K-Mart discount stores around the United States. This innovative joint venture could eventually make Ford into one of North America's largest retail banks. The plan is to open at least a further one thousand bank branches in K-Mart stores. Chrysler is also diversifying into financial services after buying Bank of America's consumer finance unit and EF Hutton's leasing business. And General Motors has acquired the Colonial Group of mortgage banking companies.

Japanese consumer electronics group Sony has sought to provide a counterbalance to its position in video recorders and CD players by diversifying into the entertainment software business. Sony established a video distribution company which diversified into the production and distribution of high quality films through Sony Pictures. Sony aims to become a world market leader in foreign and domestic theatre, home video and television markets. And it has earmarked funding to attain that objective.

Manufacturing industry already externalizes many of its services. Where volume of business is insufficient, new service companies can benefit from the search for increased efficiency and profitability. Where volume is large, the captive market will justify diversification - as noted in the U.S. automotive industry. According to Price Waterhouse, the development of in-house software in industry is decreasing continuously throughout the world: from 55% in 1985, this figure dropped to 50% in 1990 and will probably be no more than 40% by 1995.

Meanwhile, European car manufacturers are not sitting idle. Apart from the number of leasing companies established by each manufacturer and car rental firms to boost marque visibility and sales, Volvo goes one step further than just having its own bank.

A large share of the value added created in industry is services to production. Volvo illustrates this. The car manufacturer buys an estimated ECU 300 million of services per year. This car company also diversifies into new services on the basis of "intangible" features: after all, Volvo is best known for safety and reliability. Accordingly, the company is reported to be offering its consultancy services to other automotive manufacturers to help them make "safe" cars.

Volvo has acquired 20% of the shares of Park Ridge Corporation, the holding company of Hertz, the world's leading car rental company. Hertz manages a fleet of 400,000 cars worldwide, employs 30,000 persons and invests each year ECU 1.8 billion in new cars. By taking this share in Park Ridge, Volvo hopes to sell an additional 5,000 Volvos per year to the rental company. Volvo Sweden has for years controlled the Hertz operation in Sweden.

Manufacturing industry's productivity improvements depend on increasing productivity at the level of services content. Given that approximately 75% of the value added created in industry is in respect of services to production, it follows that new production methods, scrap control, quality programmes and the like will improve productivity with respect to only 25% of the value added. The remainder will hinge on enhanced services productivity.

In many ways, services are emerging as vital competitive tools for large manufacturing companies.

General Motors' competitive position is largely determined by its capacity to manage information worldwide about suppliers, new technologies, exchange rates, swap potentials, and market shifts. GM, through GMAC, has found financial services an indispensable competitive weapon in the marketplace.

Today, it is hard to imagine an engineer designing a complex solution without recourse to software. As a result, traditional industrial engineering concerns are shifting to software development. The German market, to name but one, offers several examples. AEG, the electrical appliance group, owns AEG Software-Technik (AST). Thyssen Industries has a controlling share of Ikoss. Krupp Atlas Datasystems is the sofware division of the Krupp Group. BMW controls Softlab. Daimler Benz is investing in SOGETI, the holding which controls Cap Gemini Sogeti. Daimler-Benz announced in July 1991 the biggest scoop: it acquired de facto control of Europe's largest software services group Cap Gemini Sogeti. Interesting to note: the first division of the software group which falls under direct control of Daimler Benz is the newly established Gemini Consulting.

Most of these diversifications are not readily apparent from statistics, which are usually given for the industry as a whole.

Services offer a rich new array of channels through which manufacturers can reach specialized market segments. Electronic home shopping and interactive video terminals located in banks, airports, hotels, airplanes and shopping malls allow manufacturers to make contact with a whole new set of customers in situations where potential clients are more likely to buy. Similar technology installed in retail showrooms allows potential customers to scan the full range of a manufacturer's products - which individual retailers could not possibly carry due to limitations of space.

Services can permit manufacturers to be much more responsive to fluctuating or one-off demand patterns. Manufacturing success today often turns on more rapid feedback from the marketplace, better customized products, and more efficient delivery within a shorter time span. All this is dependent on services to the production industry. Thus, by the simple expedient of affixing bar code labels to its jeans range, Levi's is now able to provide replenishment of stock for retailers three times faster than its Asian competitors.

The computer industry in particular must offer increasingly efficient delivery in shorter time cycles for a clientele which is predominantly drawn from fast-moving services companies. Texas Instruments even brings its sales personnel for custom-designed chips into the customers' premises to help them develop new products and applications. The Texas Instruments argument runs: "Silicon is the vehicle, but service is the product".

Services affect manufacturing most significantly in its international operations. The real economies of scale that transnational manufacturing companies most often enjoy are due in substantial measure to service capabilities - e.g., technology transfer, marketing skills, financial services, logistics, information networks, security, archiving, quality cleaning - rather than to plant operating economies. Indeed, while direct labour, materials and plant overheads tend to drop markedly with offshore manufacture, logistics tend to increase by 20%. So important are these costs that Japanese car producers establish U.S. ventures only after they have determined the most cost-effective logistics system. Since most other costs of manufacturing in the United States and in Japan are essentially fixed costs, logistical services have become the key strategic variable.

That said, industry often follows a core product strategy and sells off its product related services. In 1991, Johnson Wax, a leading manufacturer of cleaning products, sold its service operation in the United States to ISS. Electrolux, the large Swedish manufacturer of white goods, sold all its cleaning and laundry operations to ISS and Rentokil and, in Brazil, Electrolux invited the management of the cleaning operations to take over the business. Reckitt-Colman has also retreated from the market by selling service operations to BET, to Group 4 Securitas and to ISS.

Twinning for growth is not merely a slogan highlighting the fact that the competitive edge and, thus, the bottom line of industry depend on the integration of new, innovative and often sophisticated services. Twinning for growth also refers to the need to form alliances: the world's market leader in cleaning establishes close ties and even joint manufacturing programmes with the number one soap producer. After all, who has the best experience in cleaning?

To conclude, we should not forget that both public sector and private sector services should consider twinning. After all, if there is one area where the public is convinced of bad service, it is all too often precisely in the area of public services. There are innumerable opportunities for the private sector to collaborate with the public sector to offer private citizens the service that they want at a price/ quality relation that is within reason.

This is not a plea for straightforward privatization. It is not a contribution to the public vs. private debate. It is a comment based on the need to serve the client. Over the past few years, hospitals in the United Kingdom have been up for privatization. In more than 50% of cases, the hospital management has remained in the hands of the local authorities for the simple reason that they made the best offer...

CHAPTER FIVE

Services: A Booming World Market

Services nowadays account for well over 50% of the world's economic output. Services trade, notoriously underestimated in official statistics, is well over a quarter of trade in goods. Some 40% of worldwide foreign direct investment is now in service activities.

As we have seen, services companies have been achieving double-digit growth rates and are helping manufacturing industry to be more competitive at a time when the socio-economic environment as a whole seems to have come to terms with the notion of zero or very low growth, at least for the advanced economies. Worse, we also seem to have accepted that unemployment is a fact that we simply must learn to live with.

One can be forgiven for asking, however, how it is possible that, while manufacturing industry and even financial services are characterized by a continuous loss of jobs and agriculture is absorbing billions in subsidies, technology has not proven itself to be a panacea? Although no one will question the importance of recent breakthroughs such as in electronics, optics, new materials and biogenetics, it is clear that the unemployment problem cannot be solved by accumulating new inventions and new technologies.

Taken together, Europe, North America and Australasia need to generate an estimated 90 million jobs between now and the turn of the century. In the Third World, the corresponding figure is above one billion.

Which sector of the economy can best respond to these challenges?

The answer is "Services".

There are some 25 European entrepreneurs who have changed the shape of the world market for services. They generated some 750,000 jobs and ECU 25 billion in turnover. Their capital needs were often negligible, not one of them started his or her first company with more than ECU 100,000. While some of the companies mentioned have not yet reached the billion ECU mark, these entrepreneurs turned executives have left their stamp on the business in which they clearly take a leadership role.

Table 5-1.   Top 25 of European Service Entrepreneurs which shape the world market for services (1965-1990)

Or how 25 persons succeeded in creating 750,000 jobs in 20 years, generating approximately ECU 25 billion in turnover and maintaining double-digit growth.

Poul Andreassen	cleaning	ISS	DK
Pierre Bellon	catering	Sodexho	F
Silvio Berlusconi	media	Fininvest	I
Richard Branson	entertainment	Virgin	UK
Miguel Duran	lotteries	ONCE	E
Tom Farmer	car repair	Kwik Fit	UK
Ph. Foriel-Destezet	temporary employment	ECCO	F
Giorgio Giugiario	design	Italdesign	I
Frits Goldschmeding	temps/security	Randstad	NL
Bertil Hult	language training	EF	S/USA
Serge Kampf	software	Cap Gemini Sogeti	F
Bessel Kok	financial telecom	S.W.I.F.T.	B
Henry Lavanchy	temporary employment	Adia	CH
Robert Maxwell	publishing	MCC	UK
Reinhard Mohn	publishing	Bertelsmann	G
Claus Møller	training	TMI	DK
Werner Otto	mail order	Otto Versand	G
J. Philip-Sørensen	security	Group 4 Securitas	NL/S
Jan Pierre	international moving	Arthur Pierre	B
Glen Renfrew	electronic publishing	Reuters	UK
Hilsdon Ryan	fast consumer services	Minit Int'l	B/CH
Clive Thompson	pest control	Rentokil	UK/DK
Gilbert Trigano	tourism	Club Med	F
Nicholas Wills	business support services	BET	UK
Egon Zehnder	executive search	Egon Zehnder	CH

Source: author's research, 1991

In the world market for services is it remarkable to see how many of the leading services entrepreneurs are European. An American top ten of leading business-men who have made an impact on the services industry is as follows:

Table 5-2.   **Top of American services entrepreneurs**

Michael D. Eisner	The Walt Disney Company
Mitchell Fromstein	Manpower Temporary Services
William H. Gates III	MicroSoft
Lester Korn and Richard Ferry	Korn Ferry International
J.W. Marriott	Marriott Corporation
Joseph Neubauer	ARA Services Inc.
William Pollard	ServiceMaster
James D. Robinson III	American Express
Fred W. Smith	Federal Express
Ted Turner	CNN

Source: author's research, 1991

The Job Machine

Economy-wide employment growth is due to a dramatic rise in services sector employment, which more than compensates for the decline in the manufacturing sector. These divergent trends have now finally put an end to the notion that manufacturing is the primary force of every economy. Growth in the service sector has proceeded and will continue to proceed largely independently of the evolution of manufacturing, notwithstanding the fact that manufacturing tradi-tionally generates more indirect jobs per direct job than the service sector.

What are the factors that have been causing these changes? This is the question which two American researchers, Mr. P. Israilevich (in *Economic Perspectives*, April 1991, Federal Reserve Bank of Chicago) and R. Madidhara (University of Illinois) have attempted to answer through a brief study of employment patterns in the metropolitan area of Chicago.

Differential trends in job creation might be ascribed to greater productivity increases in manufacturing than in service jobs. Another explanation might be that manufacturing firms contract out jobs previously done in-house, so that employment that used to be classified as manufacturing enters into service jobs categories. That is what industrial economists usually argue.

The main reason is simple: there is a change in the composition of final demand. For example, the ageing population in modern economies - on the whole relatively well off - demands more personal services such as health care and specific leisure services but less sporting equipment, thus causing differential rates of employment creation. Furthermore, the increasing participation of women in the labour force increases the demand for personal and business services such as day care, restaurants, dry cleaning. This amounts to contracting-out at the domestic level similar to that towards personal and business services in manufacturing.

The increasing sophistication of all production processes, both in goods and services, has certainly also stimulated the need for expertise that comes mostly in the form of service activities. Finally, the number of portable services (i.e., transportable over distance) and that of durable services (i.e., services that retain their value and usability over time) has been rising strongly. In the management consultancy sector, for example, pension plan schemes can be provided at a distance. Most software packages are durable services.

The research referred to above throws light on these issues. It shows that out-sourcing by manufacturing has only played a modest role in the expansion of employment in the service sector. Differential rates of progress in labour productivity as between manufacturing and services also appear to have accounted for little in the divergent trends in employment creation. The significant growth in employment in the service sector overall seems to have been primarily due to changing composition of final demand that comes in addition to the expanding size of the demand coming with growth of the economy. Not unexpectedly, at the sectoral level, the most dramatic impact of changes in final demand has been in the personal and business services sectors.

In the European Community (nine Member States) between 1970 and 1985, service employment (both market and non-market) increased from 46% to 60% of the active population; that percentage went up to 65% in 1989. In other words, out of ten working people, at least six had a job classified in the service sector. The EC is slightly ahead of Japan but behind the United States, where eight workers out of ten are in the tertiary sector. The most striking features come out in an assessment of net creation of employment. In the European Community (nine Member States), from 1970 to 1986, agriculture lost 5.6 million jobs and industry 10.3 million, while services gained 17 million jobs.

It is the business services sector which has been the most dynamic segment of the tertiary sector. Its share is still small but growing fast. Consultancy and research, legal services, engineering, information and telecommunication, advertising, sales promotion, temporary work, quality control and inspection, security services and contract cleaning are some of the major components of this tertiary industry segment. A wide spectrum of service companies do grow at spectacular double-digit rates, which is to say 30 or 40% per year, and have doubled their turnover every three years for over a decade.

The first reason which enables those companies to do the impossible - or what would appear, at least, to be impossible - is that they have positioned themselves in niche markets which have themselves grown at spectacular rates. What is more, they have a management style and culture which makes optimal use of market opportunities.

What other explanation can there be for the fact that, in all the OECD countries combined, private service companies created a staggering 21.3 million new jobs between 1976 and 1983? All the more remarkable, incidentally, that this came during a crisis period characterised by efforts to combat inflation and to recover from the impact of two oil shocks.

This growth translates as an increase of 17.7% per year. By contrast, the number of new jobs created in the public services sector was a mere 4 million over the corresponding reference period. The European OECD countries added 5.1 million jobs in private services, double the job gains in the public sector.

Since 1978, the services sector has provided the highest number of jobs in every European Community country. And growth in services employment has been sustained over the last fifteen years.

A report on employment trends from 1986 to 1990 released by the U.K. Institute of Manpower Studies estimates a rise of 540,000 jobs in services as compared with a fall of 665,000 in farming and manufacturing industries. For example, over the twelve-month period from April 1986 through March 1987, there were 341,000 new jobs created in the services sector in the United Kingdom, whereas manufacturing industry shed 130,000 jobs over the same reference period.

In the United Kingdom, manufacturing now accounts for just over one in five jobs; this compares with one in three in 1966. The future for the services sector seems bright indeed.

The services sector in Spain was responsible for over one million new jobs - some 280 new jobs a day - between 1976 and 1986. Unfortunately, manufacturing industry, agriculture and construction shed 1.7 million jobs over the same period. The net result was, clearly, an increase in overall unemployment, with Spain's jobless young ranking among the highest in Europe. In 1990, services represented 54.5% of all jobs in Spain; this compared with 41.6% only fifteen years earlier.

Over the same "crisis" period, Belgium created 500,000 new jobs in services, of which two thirds are in the private sector. Concurrently, 150,000 individuals decided to establish an independent (i.e., self-employed) business operation, again, almost exclusively offering services.

The trend shows no sign of abating. Employment in services soared from 75 million in 1986 to 85.3 million in 1990. During the same period the number of jobs in the goods sector stagnated, moving from 24.6 million to 25 million.

Statistics on services in Japan appear to document a relatively low level of development. But these statistics are misleading.

The Japanese Tidal Wave

In a previous book ('The Second Wave') by this author, an attempt was made to evaluate and dissect Japan's approach to the world market for services. At the time of publication, there was considerable scepticism as to the analysis. Some critics took the line that Japan may have been successful on the manufacturing industry front, but would not be at all capable of transposing that approach to services - not least of the financial variety.

The *Financial Times*, in its review of *The Second Wave*, could see no proof that Japan was poised to capture the world market for financial services. The critic felt the book was insufficiently documented. The most recent market trends demonstrate convincingly that Japan is doing precisely that. Japan has developed a keen interest in services, has targeted its strategies to specific high value-added services and has advanced quickly in those segments of the services market it has identified as priority areas.

While manufacturing continues to grow impressively, the output of Japan's services sector is growing even faster - by over 30% between 1986 and 1990. The pace now is largely set by the whole of Japan's tertiary sector: transport, utilities, finance, property and distribution as well as business and private services.

Until 1987 or 1988, investment in the services sector accounted for half of all investment in Japan. Now it accounts for up to two thirds. And, thanks to this heavier investment, productivity in Japan's service sector has been growing at an annual rate of close to 4%, more than twice as fast as elsewhere.

Japan's service sector now accounts for 63% of GNP.

Since 1987, 75% of Japanese investment abroad has been in services. This large non-manufacturing component principally reflects the expansion of Japanese financial companies overseas. Financial and insurance companies accounted for 32% of total outward investment.

After financial services, Japan has been moving abroad vigorously in retailing, restaurants, leasing and travel. Other sectors, including education, advertising and communication are following. They may well succeed because the companies seeking to provide world-beating services are benefitting from the same advantages and using the same factors that gave Japan an edge in its successful export industries. They enjoy a docile, well trained and hard-working labour force that is comparatively poorly paid.

Even the most cursory analysis of those services where the Land of the Rising Sun has taken on the mantle of world leadership suggests that Japanese service companies excel in market segments which exhibit the following elements:

Table 5-3.   Strategic approach to services: a comparison between Europe and Japan

JAPAN	EUROPE
High-volume business	Low unit volume
Highly standardized services	Customized
Central importance of the home market	International markets
Highly price sensitive services	High value added
Dependent on hi-tech application	Human resources dependent

Source: author 1987

It emerges that there are clear niches in which Europeans currently hold the advantage. And, in turn, those enable us to identify areas where we can look forward to fierce competition from Japanese business.

At the same time, penetrating the Japanese market presents a unique challenge. Europe has clear opportunities for services which are linked to the new life style and to personnel. As a rule of thumb, the author believes that European companies in Japan should focus their efforts on services which are human capital related, offered in low volume and with a high value-added content. Further, the focus could best be on services which exhibit little price sensitivity.

Several companies have proven that this approach has more than just theory to commend it. Adia, Time Manager International, Egon Zehnder, Minit International, S.W.I.F.T., CEDEL, Reuters, DHL, SGS, Giorgio Giugiario, Maxwell Infoline, Inchcape are not only successful in Japan, they often hold a leading (and profitable) market share in that country.

We have become accustomed to European and U.S. moves against Japanese trading practices in the manufacturing sector; we now seem to be positioning ourselves for a decade of disagreement with Japan as regards "unfair trading practices" in the services sector.

Japanese distribution has often been discounted as inefficient, and as one of the main reasons for the lack of success of Western exports to Japan.

As a matter of fact, one out of four Japanese is employed in distribution. On the other hand, it is difficult to justify the claim that a system involving anything up to six to eight intermediaries between the production and the consumer is efficient.

Not surprisingly, however, distribution in Japan is undergoing a radical reappraisal. The leading Japanese supermarkets and department stores are clearly positioning themselves for international expansion.

In the 1960s and 1970s, Japanese department stores concluded a series of cooperation agreements with famous stores in Europe and the United States in order to coordinate imports of foreign quality products via the purchasing departments of leading groups such as Sears (USA), Kaufhof (Germany), Marks and Spencer (United Kingdom), Au Printemps (France) and KF (Sweden). Subsequently, several Japanese retailers invited leading European and North American groups to join in the launching of new outlets in Japan.

It may well be that Japan has some way to go in streamlining its distribution activities. It may also be true that Japan does not possess the *flair* for services that we in the Western Hemisphere believe we have acquired over the years. When all is said and done, however, there can no longer be any doubt that the Japanese are attacking the services sector with the same dedication and commitment that they have previously shown in key areas of manufacturing industry such as steel, shipbuilding, electronics and automobiles.

As suggested earlier, it is surely time to take their growing presence in services very seriously indeed.

One thing is certain, the Japanese are actively learning from our strengths in services. Nomura Research Institute - the largest research outfit in the world - has commissioned studies on several sectors which have been outlined in this book and even added one: the HIMS or highly intelligent and mobile services. According to the Japanese, Europe is a world market leader in the commercialization of HIMS. The only problem the Japanese had while conducting this research, was that the Europeans were not aware of this "fact".

In fact, Japan itself has a very well-developed services sector, particularly in the form of services to industry. For statistical purposes, however, Japan subsumes these services into "manufacturing".

When all is said and done, Japan's competitive edge derives in large measure from its very efficient production processes which include - according to recent calculations - between 70 and 75% producer services. The Japanese have also recognized that further increases in productivity in manufacturing industry will stem from improvements in services productivity.

The pattern the Japanese see for their economic future is something between an economy based on manufacturing and one based on services. Mr. Tadahiro Sekimoto, president of NEC and an ardent advocate of this manufacturing/ services mix, calls it the "two-and-a-half industry stage", because enterprises such as his are halfway between the secondary and tertiary sectors.

Before the end of the century, Japanese industry will switch an estimated two million jobs from manufacturing to services. Overall, the economy will have to find an additional 8.2 million jobs.

Between 1986 and 1990, twenty-five Japanese service sectors exhibited double-digit growth. European and U.S. services companies should bear in mind that these are all sectors where Western companies *at present* enjoy a clear competitive edge over Japan.

The twenty-five sectors include:

* Temporary employment services (up 30% per annum)
* Courier services (up 18%)
* Training and education (up 24%)
* Credit card services (up 11%)
* Leasing and rental (up 27%)
* Removals (up 13%)
* Sports (excluding golf courses) (up 16%)
* Amusement and theme parks (up 12%)
* Health care services (up 14%); and
* Information services (up 19%).

Whereas Japan has clearly succeeded in taking over market shares in products, they have failed in many services, the financial services being the main exception until now. In the European information technology market for example, Japan (and the Four Tigers) controls 42% of chips, 40% of OEM but only 1% of IT (information-technology)-related services. But, as the bottom line shifts from manufacturing to services-related turnover, the Japanese will not sit still. After all, EDS is 20% controlled by Hitachi.

Singapore's services sector is likely to spearhead the country's economic expansion over the next decade. This is the view of an expert panel in a report to the government's special Economic Committee set up in 1986 to chart the island's growth. The Economic Development Board's advisory committee had recommended that the services sector be promoted alongside manufacturing as a second engine of growth in the economy.

Singapore's Economic Development Board has indeed started promoting the services sector. In 1985, medical services yielded gross receipts of some ECU 126 million, with a value added of ECU 27,600 per worker. The value of computer services rose from ECU 27.6 million in 1980 to ECU 227 million in 1985, and is expected to generate ECU 1.6 billion by 1995. Education services generate an annual revenue of ECU 38.2 million. Laboratory and testing services account for ECU 40.6 million and a value-added per worker of ECU 6,918.

These four, together with some nine other services, have been designated target growth areas for the Singapore economy. Even if concrete and detailed strategies have yet to be fully articulated, this marks a first targeted strategy for the development of new comparative advantages in services.

The promotion of services has never been more crucial to Singapore's economic growth. In effect, the sector could grow at 7% annually for the next ten years. For example, Singapore is investing heavily in its health care services to inject new impetus into the economy. As a part of a more concerted shift towards services, the Economic Committee has pinpointed medicare as a sunrise services sector. Medical services are highly productive and generate substantial amounts of foreign exchange. Exports, in the form of medical treatment for foreigners, totalled ECU 79.9 million in 1984 and could reach an estimated ECU 400 million by 1994.

Singapore already has the highest ratio of service exports to GDP in the world: 54.1 % compared to a world average of 3.7 %.

Small is beautiful.

Tunisia, another small country, has also embarked on a programme to export services. In 1990, the country exported 12,400 professionals throughout French-speaking Africa, the Maghreb and the Middle East. Ten years ago, there were only 1,000 Tunisians abroad under this special programme. A local surplus of highly educated nationals, ranging from engineers to medical doctors and qualified security guards, capable of mastering French, Arabic and often even English, has provided a significant export opportunity. These qualified persons are increasingly replacing European expatriates, who are less willing to work in so-called "hardship" posts. What is more, it has replaced them for as little as half to one-third of their cost.

Entrepreneurship in Services

Another key factor is that the healthiest economies are also the most turbulent. They attract the highest levels of start-ups, but they also tend to exhibit the greatest number of company failures - even if the overall impact is to maximize job creation.

Today, about 1.4 million new businesses are being created in North America each year, compared with 90,000 in 1950. Over the next three years, small and medium-sized companies in the United Kingdom will increase their employment by 700,000, whereas some 300,000 persons will become self-employed. The Belgian Small Business Research Institute has published a report showing that almost all of Belgium's job gains during the first four years of the 1980s came from start-ups with less than five persons. Only very few of these companies were in the high-tech business, and nearly all new employment was found in "new services". Every year, some 40,000 new businesses open in Belgium, a proof of entrepreneurship as an important basis for the development of new competitive advantages.

Traditionally, wage levels in services may have appeared on average lower than in manufacturing industry. But, today, services provide the most promising opportunity for new workers with little experience, part-timers, high school students, women and retirees entering or re-entering the workforce.

When assessing wage conditions in services, one should adjust for these entry conditions, the more convenient working environment, the lower experience requirements and the more flexible working hours offered by many services jobs. Such jobs are essential for multiple-earner families; they are also a valuable platform for the development of attitudes, skills and disciplines needed for other jobs.

Unlike in manufacturing industry, barely qualified people *do* have career prospects in professional services companies. In manufacturing, a cleaner or a security guard will tend to stay in that job for life.

The employment structure in services is also fundamentally different from manufacturing. In the leisure services, 40% of all employees work less than 35 hours per week, 17% are younger than 20 years old, and women represent 40% of the total. In manufacturing industry, an average 9% work less than 40 hours, only 4% are younger than 20, and women represent 32% of the workforce.

These figures speak for themselves - although they are invariably overlooked.

Trade in Services: The Right Concepts

A second major indicator of the growth perspectives for services resides in the fact that services are becoming *tradeable* for the first time in history.

Here, another range of opportunities pushes this sector, previously confined within national boundaries, down the road towards double-digit growth.

Only 8% of total services produced are traded, as compared to 45% for manufactured goods and 65% for agriculture. If services attain within the next

20 years a tradeability, transportability and storability equal to those of goods, then the sector will consistently record double-digit growth across the board.

The key role services play in the globalization of world markets and the expansion of world trade began to be recognized in the late 1980s when it appeared that in previous years exports of commercial services had been expanding twice as fast as exports of merchandise.

The latest annual publication of the GATT secretariat in Geneva (March 1991), contains preliminary figures for 1990. After having risen by 9 % in 1989, world trade in commercial services increased by an estimated 12 % in 1990 to a new high of ECU 626 billion. During the same two years, the growth of trade (value) in merchandise rose from 7.5 % to 13 %, totalling about ECU 2.8 trillion. In recent years, trade in services has accounted for somewhat more than one-fifth of the value of world trade. However, these figures do not take account of a significant statistical downward bias in service trade figures

The most important source of under-reporting of services is the fact that many service transactions are simply not registered, as is for example often the case with services transmitted electronically or when central bank records are used and there is no financial intermediary involved in the transaction. Other serious problems arise from the fact that affiliate-parent trade is very difficult to capture, as often there are no associated payments flows. Also, service statistics are often reported on a net (exports minus imports) rather than a gross basis. Another major source of underestimation is that transactions including both goods and services are typically assigned to the goods sector; this may well have become more important now that services tend increasingly to be bundled with the sale of manufactured products. Even on the basis of such incomplete data, trade in all commercial services is now twice as large as trade in mining products, and nearly twice as large as trade in agricultural products.

Many European states occupied key places among world commercial service exporters in 1989. According to GATT sources, the United States came first, France was second, immediately followed by the United Kingdom and Germany. Japan was fifth. Compared to 1980, the only ranking change was the switch between France and the United Kingdom for (respectively) the second and third place. During that same year, Japan was the leading importer of commercial services, followed by the United States and Germany.

Technological advances in service industries and progress in communications stimulate international trade in goods and indeed services themselves and transform its nature. In a world in which levels of technological sophistication are rising continuously, access to competitively priced producer services are of cardinal importance for the overall ability of industry and agriculture to compete at home and abroad. In that sense, trade in producer services may well be the major means for transferring technology, knowhow and knowledge. By offering

Table 5-4.	Leading Invisible Earners, by component, 1987		
Rank Transport	Travel	Investment income	Other services
1 USA	Spain	USA	France
2 France	USA	UK	Germany
3 Japan	Italy	Japan	UK
4 Germany	France	Belgium	USA
5 UK	UK	France	Italy
6 Netherlands	Austria	Germany	Japan
7 Italy	Germany	Switzerland	Belgium
8 Norway	Switzerland	Netherlands	Netherlands
9 Belgium	Canada	Italy	Switzerland
10 Spain	Mexico	Canada	Canada

Source: British Council for Invisible Earnings, London, 1991

exactly the same service at the same quality levels and in the same form in all parts of the world, service companies providing producer services contribute to the improvement of the export performance of firms wherever located, even those that do not enjoy the support of fully developed domestic service industries. Thus, services available on world markets reduce inequalities in opportunities between firms in countries with different levels of development.

EC Trade in Services with the Rest of the World

The European Community is the largest single trading entity for goods. In export of services (intra-EC trade not included) it is ahead of the United States. With credits in services with third countries in 1988 at ECU 118 billion and debits at ECU 108 billion, it registered a positive balance of ECU 10.3 billion. This is equivalent to two thirds of its surplus in goods. Internal trade in services is estimated to be about the same size as external trade.

In 1988, transport accounted for 35% and travel for 24% of all EC services trade. The share of what is called "Other market services" was 40%. The main items in this category for which figures are available include "trade earnings", "banking", "business services" and "construction and engineering", plus a residual category called "other".

An extrapolation of the trade in services of the Community up to 1990 suggests that in that year it may have generated a trade surplus of some ECU 17 billion. There have probably been deficits of more than ECU 1 billion in sectors such as sea freight, communication services and property income, and a surplus of 1 to 2 billion in such sectors as travel, air passenger transport, air freight, banking, construction and engineering, cultural services and in the residual "other" category.

In 1989, the U.K. private sector produced an overall current account surplus of ECU 10 billion. Of this total, financial institutions and insurance contributed ECU 9.2 billion. Approximately ECU 1.6 billion of services trade was contributed by overseas consultancy projects and ECU 520 million from the export of legal advice, a sharp increase on previous years. In the same year, the United Kingdom earned an estimated ECU 1 billion by offering English language courses to foreigners.

Tradeable service activities now account for 45% of total employment in the United Kingdom, up from only 36% in 1980. This breaks down as 12% for banking, finance and insurance, 4% for transport and telecommunications, 5% for hotels and catering, and 24% for other and new services.

France ranks second among the world's exporters of commercial services with 10.6%, right after the USA with 11.2% (1987). It now earns more foreign exchange through the organization of trade fairs and exhibitions in Paris than by exporting cars.

Accordingly to the GATT, Western Europe now accounts for 58% of world trade in commercial services. Even when some U.S. service companies are landmarks and will maintain their leadership over years to come, we may not permit ourselves to be complacent about our present competitive position versus Japan. The recent acquisition of 20% of DHL International by Japan Airlines in collaboration with Lufthansa and the ensuing battle between Reuters and Quick confirm this clearcut strategy.

Services in Eastern Europe

Even the USSR has not been able to remain indifferent towards a reconversion of the economy based on services.

The Soviet Union plans to retrench up to 20 million people from its manufacturing and agricultural workforces by the end of the century. According to Leonid Albalkin, a key economic advisor to President Gorbachev, most of the displaced industrial workers will have to find jobs in services ranging from sales and repair work to education and medical care. One-fifth of the working population in industry will shift to services before the end of the century.

Today, the countries of Eastern Europe are even offering barter trade agreements whereby they exchange services for goods. The USSR buys jeans from Lee and barters with maritime freight contracts. Hungary pays the transfer of technology from Philips with software.

In the second volume of *Das Kapital*, Karl Marx defines the productive labourer as a worker who participates in the production of material commodities. In his *Theories of Surplus Value*, Marx distinguishes within the transport sector between transport of people (according to Marx an "unproductive exchange between a personal service and revenue") and the transport of goods, which increases the exchange value of the goods and is therefore considered "productive".

Scarcely surprising, therefore, that services have long been neglected in the Socialist centrally-planned economies of Eastern Europe. The dominance of "productive" activities gave rise to a material concept of national income and, by extension, to the underdevelopment of services, which are viewed as a part of national expenditures (other than trade, transport and communications). This has resulted in a relatively lower level of wages and salaries in services by comparison with manufacturing industry.

The share of services in the gross domestic product of the Socialist countries varies from around 30% in Romania to slightly over 50% in the Soviet Union. The most service-oriented economy in Central Europe is Hungary, followed by the Soviet Union and Poland, whereas the least service-oriented countries are Romania, Bulgaria and the erstwhile German Democratic Republic. Czechoslovakia lies somewhere in between these two sets of extremes.

Increased "marketization" and, to a certain extent, privatization of services will go in tandem with the spread of the restructuring reform process - *perestroika* - in each of the Eastern European states. In Hungary for example, 61% of household consumer services were performed directly by the private sector as early as 1987. Greater freedom for entrepreneurs, including small cooperatives and private professional practices, and an increase in the autonomy of enterprises and allocation of capital are preconditions for growth.

The role of services in the foreign trade of the former Socialist Bloc countries has increased substantially in recent years to the point where services now comprise an important part of overall foreign trade. Services exports receipts in Romania represent some 6% of the value of exports of goods, whereas in Hungary the figure is closer to 14% and, in Poland, it is well over 19%.

Most Central European countries show a small surplus in their trade in services. They rely heavily on income generated from shipping and forwarding, construction engineering, and licensing and patents (offered in the main to developing countries). On the other hand, they are clearly underperforming in insurance, banking and professional services. Business support services are next to non-existent.

The largest exporters of construction and engineering services are, in order of importance, the Soviet Union and Poland. Trade in banking and insurance services is very low but, in view of the restructuring of the socialist economies, including deregulation of financial services, one may expect a new impetus for growth in trade in financial services in years to come.

There are some 750 companies in 23 developed and 50 developing countries with Central European capital participation. The major investor countries are the USSR, Hungary and Poland. What is noteworthy is that almost all the companies located in developed market economies with capital participation from Eastern Europe are in services. The most important areas of activity are trading, banking, insurance, engineering, transportation and construction.

The USSR owns six banks abroad, located in five countries. Poland has eight branches, Hungary has majority stakes in two banks and representative offices in five countries. Romania has four venture banks in the West. Overall, around 70 investments in the West are related to transport services.

By 1990, there were nearly 10,000 companies with foreign participation established in Central Europe. The share of service companies in the total number of joint ventures is some 50% for Poland, two-thirds for Bulgaria and three-quarters in Hungary.

It is clear that the potential of this market is far from being exploited, in particular in the USSR. For Western service providers and investors there are promising opportunities there for all kinds of services, not only financial services and telecommunications but also for the full range of business support services. Foreign accountancy firms are involved in the privatization drive, foreign banks and investment houses take part in the creation of stock exchanges (for example Budapest and Warsaw), and scores of consultants in management and other disciplines have entered most areas of the Central European economies. Foreign investment is high in consumer and personal services (retail, hotels, tourism, recreation). Negotiations are in progress on advisory services in telecommunications, air transport, road infrastructure, etc.

The Role of Services in the Third World

Since 1970, services have contributed the largest share of the GDP of Latin America. Employment in services has kept up with this trend.

In that year, services represented 51.6% of GDP, versus 48.6% in agriculture and industry. In 1987, the figures were 56.2% and 43.8% respectively. Services grew over this period at a compound rate of 5.5%, whereas average economic growth reached 4.9% and growth in industrial production 4.1%. Over the same 15-year period, financial and business services increased their contribution to GDP by 33%.

Data entry services currently employ 4,000 workers across the Caribbean and this figure is estimated to reach 20,000 by 1992. Investment in data entry facilities depends on the telecommunications infrastructure. Jamaica has invested ECU

6.4 million in a teleport with facilities for telemarketing, airline and hotel reservations, data entry operations and offshore office services. American Airlines established Caribbean Data Services several years ago, originally only for processing ticket data. Today, it has diversified its services and now, for example, computerized taped medical data for U.S. hospitals.

The European Commission has broadened its programmes for overseas cooperation to include a transfer of service knowhow to developing countries. The Directorate General for External Relations and Trade Policy (DG I) and the Directorate General for Development Aid (DG VIII) have launched a pilot programme with the Pacto Andino (Bolivia, Colombia, Ecuador, Peru and Venezuela). The programme provides for an analysis of "producer services", i.e., services to manufacturing.

Similarly, UNCTAD under the leadership of Murray Gibbs is now helping several developing countries to design a national and regional services policy. Since 1987, expert meetings have been organized in Costa Rica, Tunisia, Mexico and the Ivory Coast to promote this objective.

India is positioning itself rapidly on the world market through its comparative advantage in software engineering. Computer programmers earn around ECU 4,500 a year and are on the whole highly productive. Tata Consultancy Services is the largest software company in India. International Informatics Solutions, another company, has direct telecom links with a British building society. CMC Ltd. is helping the London underground with transportation software.

Citicorp has established a wholly-owned subsidiary near Bombay in the Santa Cruz Electronics Export Production Zone from where it has successfully been exporting software since 1986. Western Trust and Savings of the United Kingdom had a retail financial services package developed by Tata Unisys, a large Indian software house jointly owned by Tata Industries and Unisys. Its clients include the Hong Kong and Shangai Bank, Barclays Bank, Bank of New Zealand and Citibank. In other service areas, the Raj Group, an Indian hotels chain, is present in many countries and India also produces more films than any other country in the world, earning substantial film royalties abroad.

Foreign investments in services often account for a minor share in total foreign capital inflows into developing countries. The ratio of foreign capital to newly-created jobs is therefore deceptive. But foreign capital inflows are generally complemented by tenfold local investment in the form of training of human resources and service infrastructure developments. As a result, the total new job creation in developing countries is mainly catalyzed by foreign investments in services.

More and more, developing countries understand the need for services in the development process. But both the means and the information base are lacking. Even although more than 50% of the investments in the Philippines over the past three years have been in services, the Philippine Board of Investments has only one employee out of 800 dedicated to studying the opportunities for investments in services. In this regard, Singapore is clearly the exception in pinpointing these opportunities and taking specific measures to exploit them.

Investment risk in developing countries is high. Worse, the investment insurance schemes of most OECD states have reached their respective ceilings. Services very often offer the only prospect for expanded cooperation between the North and the South.

African countries apportion a substantial component of their export revenues to the import of services. Thus, the import of services as a percentage of the import of goods varies in the Ivory Coast between 35% and 45%. In Gabon, it lies between 50 and 60%. The average for Africa as a whole has oscillated for the past ten years or so between 25 and 38%. The trade deficit for services in the Ivory Coast increased between 1975 and 1984 at an average of 17% per annum.

Services will play an increasing role in their development process.

In the first instance, this will be due to the need for services in the commercialization of agroproduce, ores and manufactured goods. The most important services relate to access to trade information systems, risk coverage mechanisms, reinsurance, and efficient communications services for importers and distributors, quality control, certification, packaging and design.

Countries in the Third World compete heavily against each other on the world market for commodities and should find ways to generate higher value added through the integration of services.

To cite a concrete example: despite the increasing demand for tropical fruits on the European and North American markets, and despite the fact that its production capacity and variety of fruits in this area is enormous, Colombia has not succeeded in establishing itself as a leader on the world market. The main obstacle to this is the lack of support services which would enable the Colombians to improve the quality of the actual crops, to target and prepare the market, and to ensure efficient distribution.

Who is willing to invest in Colombia? A country which is characterized by drug barons and guerilla warfare? The country has but one alternative to expand dramatically its export revenues: export the same amount (or even less) but integrate more value added. The export of naturally grown tropical fruits will not only respect the fragile equatorial environment, it will permit the export of goods which are in abundance and which will not hamper local supply badly needed to respond to local demand.

The key components of a Colombian twinning of fruits and services would include pre-financing of farmers, crop selection on the basis of nutritional values and taste, agronomic counselling, quality control laboratories to ensure quality crops, and "gastronomic assistance" to prepare the market (along the lines of

New Zealand producers, who helped launch the kiwi fruit by publishing cookbooks), and certification. At the same time, and in the interests of satisfactory distribution, it presupposes the introduction of sophisticated harvesting and transport technology, preservation techniques such as IQF freezing, and selective distribution (e.g., direct sales to yoghurt manufacturers, health food stores, baby food producers). This could be backed up by traditional financial services, advertising, transport, insurance, and so on. Export the same volume, but include more value added. Services make the difference!

CHAPTER SIX

Traditional Services Feel the Pinch

Much of employment in the 1960s and 1970s was generated by the traditional services sectors of banking and insurance, transport, distribution and tourism. However, it seems clear that there are few prospects and (apparently) no hope that the four traditional pillars of services will be able to absorb the huge pool of qualified labour emerging from our schools.

On the contrary, banking and insurance will certainly shed thousands of jobs over the next decade and, after a period of mergers and acquisitions, some will have to close shop. Transport and distribution will evolve into multi-model transport and distribution systems, while the demand for leisure and entertainment will face some tough and risky decisions.

Leisure and Entertainment

Europe welcomes a large number of tourists, both vacationers and business visitors. International conferences held in Europe, an important vehicle for business tourism, represent half of all conferences held worldwide.

The hotel-restaurant sector registered more rapid growth than the other sectors of tourism. The EC has approximately 140,000 hotels, representing 3.7 million rooms. There have been important changes in hotels and hotel structures during the past ten years. The sector is becoming increasingly concentrated, as is true of most traditional services and retail sectors, and is tending towards the formation of hotel chains (which are recording growth rates over 20%), voluntary groupings and associations. One of the world market leaders is the British company Trusthouse Forte, a hotel and catering services group, headed by Lord Rocco Forte, an entrepreneur in his own right.

Tourism, the major segment of the leisure service activity, is the world's third largest industry, after the oil and motor vehicle industry. Tourism accounts for 12% of the world's gross national product. The five largest earners from tourism in the world are : the USA (11 million Canadian visitors a year), Italy, Spain, France and the United Kingdom in order of importance. No surprise that Europe has set its mind on the leisure industry. There are an estimated 10 million jobs involved in the twelve EC member states and the jobs are spread out among small companies.

In Britain, tourism sustains 1.4 million jobs and 50,000 new ones are added each year. Tourism accounts for about 5% of GNP. Hotels, health and fitness centers, museums, theme parks, spectator sports, and cinemas account in the United Kingdom alone for some ECU 1.6 billion and investments for 1988 were calculated at around ECU 1.7 billion. In 1989, tourism produced ECU 24 billion for the national economy. Since 1980, the number of business visitors to the United Kingdom has risen from 2.5 million to 3.3 million (1986). Their spending rose over the same period from ECU 525 million to ECU 1.4 billion.

The Belgian market for these economic activities provides 135,000 jobs, up from 95,000 in just three years. The market is operating in a highly entrepreneural field of small leisure companies, where failure seems as common as success. Tourism in Spain is a key sector of the economy. It represents 10 % of GDP and employs an estimated 11 % of the workforce. Growth in tourism over the past five years is also reflected in an increase of about 3 % in employment per year. Fortunes have been generated over the past decade through a strategy of mass tourism. Growth in Spanish tourism levelled off in 1990.

The most important trend on the market is segmentation. Hotels are trying to provide specific packages of services to narrowly defined target groups: the business traveller, the weekend tourist, the tour operators, the airlines, government officials and diplomatic staff. Hotels try to accommodate two or more types of clients in one hotel offering them different facilities. Some hotels even provide more modest rooms, with separate entrances or floors in a separate part of the hotel for budget clients.

At the same time, given the diversity and specific character of its resources, Europe is experiencing perceptible growth in the demand for new forms of accommodation, which should result in the emergence of "unique" forms of lodging ("niche" marketing). Informal chains of hotels such as "Relais et Châteaux" and "The Leading Hotels in the World" are examples of networking. The advent of "suites only" hotels is another case in point.

The holiday market has become strongly segmented according to country, providing new forms of accommodation in response to an intensified desire to learn about a region through cultural and sports activities (holiday villages, guest houses, farms, bed and breakfast). To develop this type of tourism, transportation costs must be kept low. Cultural tourism and "travelling to learn" have even become a marketing tool for companies such as Club Med which goes as far as to offer computer courses for executives on African beaches.

Retired people with leisure time and enough money for holidays tend to travel and to remain on holiday longer than other groups. This market segment will be the fastest-growing next to business travel. Given that one person out of three in Europe will be over 55 in the year 2000, this segment of the market represents considerable potential for the hotel industry, particularly in the off-season. The permutation of tourism and health care represents a growing market niche. Tourism is one of the key leisure sectors that should benefit from a spending boom of "grey" consumers in the 1990's and thereafter. Particularly in Western Europe and Japan, where the population is ageing, those in the over 50-55 age group have comfortable disposable incomes to spend on themselves, and this is set to grow steadily over the next decade. They live longer and are in better health than the previous generations of "grey" people. These affluent people, particularly the West Europeans, seek second holidays and regular weekend breaks. All these factors can be expected to fuel leisure markets such as travel, eating out and some kinds of participatory sports.

A combination of tourism and health care is a growing market niche. There are an estimated 22 million Americans who vacation at a health spa. This service is also popular in the USSR, were 15 million Soviets take a spa holiday each year. The Spanish Tourism Office has calculated that they could increase foreign currency revenues by as much as ECU 80 million per year if they improve the quality of their 93 health spas. France has built up a first class name for spas thanks to the export of its mineral waters (Vichy, Perrier, Contrex).

These trends mark the decrease in importance of mass tourism. Margins there are low, and lately do not even reach 10 ECU per night per tourist. Risks are high in view of increasing air transport problems. In 1989, when thousands of tourists got stuck in airports because of traffic congestion, all tour operators saw their small margins wiped out by additional costs due to one-to-two day delays before departure.

The Mediterranean countries still welcome the greatest number of tourists, but growing competition represented by the Asian and African countries cannot be ignored. What is worse, the beaches of the Mediterranean no longer satisfy the diverse tastes of today's tourists, and popular countries like Italy and Spain are facing a downturn in their revenues. The worsening of pollution, especially in Italy, will certainly contribute to this trend.

The only way to secure margins is to enter into adjacent businesses, or to form alliances with strategic partners. This has generated a broader platform for competition. Several airlines have invested in hotel chains and have become major players on the market:

SAS	-	SAS Hotels
Air France	-	Le Méridien
Royal Dutch Airlines/KLM	-	Tulip Hotels

Some companies have diversified into financial services. Thomas Cook Traveller Cheques has a leading position in the world. Credit card companies like

American Express have become world leaders in travel related services; Diners Club has set up for the travelling executive a series of executive lounges at international airports. The market is on one hand specializing, on the other hand strongly embarking on diversification. Competition may come from sources one does not expect. Travel agencies are networking successfully. The Rosenbluth Group is one of the most remarkable new groupings covering the world.

France has launched itself into a new age in terms of the leisure and entertainment sectors. The average Frenchman spends FF 250 per person on a visit to an amusement park. Little surprise, then, that, in addition to France's own version of Euro Disneyland, Asterix Park and Mirapolis have sprung up near Paris, Smurf Land in Lorraine, and Futuroscope near Poitiers.

France has clearly opted for the theme park route. Its Euro-Disneyland represents a first-phase investment of ECU 2 billion. By 1992, it should be attracting 11 million visitors a year, boosting France's tourist earnings by ECU 1 billion annually and creating some 30,000 new jobs. When final rail links are in place in 1994, Brussels will be little more than an hour away, London three hours via the "Chunnel". Euro Disney expects to welcome as many as two million guests a year from Central Europe from 1995 onwards.

To its credit, the French Government was quick to recognize the enormous potential implicit in theme parks, and moved swiftly to put incentives in place: a reduction of value-added tax on entry tickets to 7% (from the usual 18%), a ECU 219 million infrastructural development programme, and concessional borrowing at rates normally reserved to French public authorities - these are only some of the generous concessions designed to promote the concept. In return, France acquires its own Disney World where French is the *lingua franca*.

The French have clearly not been insensitive to the fact that Walt Disney leisure and entertainment group profits have risen by a minimum of 25 % per annum from fiscal year 1986 through fiscal year 1990, with operating income from home video products and services based on cartoon characters such as Mickey Mouse and Donald Duck spiralling 134 %, filmed entertainment revenues up 109 %, and direct income from theme parks and resorts up 31 %.

Another segment of the leisure industry which has been booming is cruising. According to Lloyd's Register of Shipping, in the spring of 1991 there were more than 80 new cruise ships on order worldwide, a number unheard of since the days of transatlantic liner travel. Growth has been driven principally by the North American market, especially in the Caribbean, the world's premier cruise destination. That market alone now accounts for close to 4 million passengers a year, not all North Americans. European cruises, mostly in the Mediterranean, have recently been picking up strongly but from a lower base. Cruising in South-East Asia has yet to develop significantly.

Cruise operators exploit the trend towards more frequent but shorter holidays and offer plenty of three-to-five-day cruises, the fastest growing segment of the market. The cost of ships is often reduced by subsidies provided by some governments keen to keep their shipyards busy.

Whereas tourism has succeeded in becoming a leading employer and forex generator, the potential for quantum growth is limited. The amount of capital needed increases and the skills of employees required today is not comparable with those required just a decade ago. The only market which may very well upset the present trends is the Japanese market. The Japanese government has come to the conclusion that perhaps the only way to cope with the greying of the population is to export the elderly and secure health care, entertainment, food and maintenance services in sun-rich regions of the world. The Mediterranean has been selected as one of those potential regions.

Distribution

The erosion of boundaries between traditional sectors has meant that they will have to find new markets in order to maintain their present level of employment. Distribution is up for innovation, and success will accrue to those who identify gaps in the marketplace.

Marks and Spencer, one of Britain's largest retail stores groups, has been granted a licence to take deposits by the Bank of England. The new licence is granted to St. Michael Financial Services, the group's financial subsidiary, which administers the store's independent charge card. Turnover in financial services has tripled from 1987 through 1991. Since launching the card in 1987, Marks and Spencer has signed up 33 million holders. This is yet another sign of the steady convergence between retailing and banking. Marks and Spencer cardholders largely outnumber those of both Diners Club and American Express in the United Kingdom.

Thanks to the quality of the customer database, Marks & Spencer has successfully expanded its range of financial services to include broker/dealer transactions in the shares of publicly traded companies.

The advent of store cards demonstrates how retailers are challenging the banks' and the brokers' traditional role. Some stores even sell unit trusts and life insurance. Finance is now as much a part of department store life as underwear. Marks and Spencer invested ECU 52 million in its computer centre operation which employs 450 information technology experts. The group is internationalizing fast. It has opened a fifth store in Paris, it has five stores in Hong Kong, and has acquired Brooks Brothers and Kings Supermarkets in the United States. In 1991, M & S turnover increased by 3% and profits broke the ECU 920 million mark, up 6 % compared with one year earlier.

The boundaries between traditional services are eroding as new alliances and schemes of cooperation are set up. The BBC has signed an agreement with Marks and Spencer for the distribution of its video series, a selection drawn from the world's largest non-commercial film library.

The U.K. Post Office, the world's oldest service infrastructure, is also reappraising its strengths in an effort to increase productivity. In the Netherlands, the Postbank was launched with a total balance sheet of ECU 13 billion. It quickly merged with the Nederlandse Middenstands Bank (NMB) to form one of the most successful private/public partnerships. And the U.S. Post Office now markets the white border on its stamps as advertising space.

Productivity in retailing depends on the merger between EFTPOS technology and computer-aided store design. W.H. Smith, the U.K. records, magazines and books high-street chain, has invested ECU 325,000 in forging a link between EFTPOS and CAD (computer aided design). The W.H. Smith system can create customer profiles and analyze how they perceive and are attracted to goods on display. An EFTPOS link permits translation of the value of every product line into an electronic image, attributing a sales value to every square metre of store interior and maximizing space utilization with a degree of accuracy hitherto impossible. Productivity enhancement is assessed at more than 2% of gross profits.

The Financial World Under Pressure

It has been estimated that commercial banking's work force in the United States will drop this decade by 20%, or 300,000 jobs. Cutbacks are taking place across the board, but hit hardest are employees in clerical operations, which account for 60% of a bank's costs. Two mergers Chemical Bank and Manufacturers Hanover in New York and NCNB and C&S Sovran in Southeast USA will cost at least 15,000 employees their jobs. The acquisition of Security Pacific by BankAmerica will go the same way. Citicorp has already cut 7,000 employees and recently indicate it may eliminate as many as 10,000 more jobs, while Chase Manhattan Corp has reduced payroll by 5,000. For many bankers who survive the budget cuts, the specter of a business in decline has created a culture of fear and uncertainty. Some banks fare remarkably well. The Royal Bank of Canada has crunched out a ECU 500 million profit even in adverse circumstances. The leading retail bank of North America seems well prepared for the 90s.

In many ways, bankers are facing the same fate as farmers, steelworkers, coal miners and others who have been replaced by technology and affected by consolidation. The 1.7 million-strong bank European employees' union based in Geneva has exerted pressure on banks to invest in new activities in order to sustain present levels of employment.

Deutsche Bank leads the way. It purchased a 24% stake in Roland Berger,

Germany's largest independent management consultancy and raised its holding to 75.1% by the end of 1988. Roland Berger, founded in 1967, has twenty-one partners and a total staff of 250. Deutsche Bank is convinced that consultancy is the third branch of business it must develop after commercial and investment banking. Incidentally, the bank already holds 4.9% of the capital of U.K. merchant bank Morgan Grenfell and 33% of the Tokyo consulting firm Vaubel & Partners.

Two thirds of Europe's banks now offer home banking services. In 1992, nearly 90% of the 400 leading European banks will be in a position to do so.

The main reason for offering home banking is to improve productivity. The main obstacle to its further development is consumer resistance and the limited availability of sufficiently cheap home electronics.

As new technologies and automation in the services sector become more visible to the consumer, so too will be the increasing need for reassurance that "the company cares". In a ECU 4 million campaign, Barclays Bank of the United Kingdom, for example, launched a TV commercial on the theme of the high-tech society where individual and friendly service is still paramount. Barclays backs this up with a more open bank design and additional, non-cashier staff available to help with general banking inquiries.

Dai-Ichi Kangyo and seven other banks have linked their smart cards into Fujitsu's communications network. Sanwa Bank and 86 other companies, including JCB, Japan's largest credit card, have launched a project that not only enables the client to credit, cash and debit his account, but also to engage in catalogue shopping from the office and check in automatically at selected hotels in Tokyo and Osaka.

The market for insurance services has been increasing at double-digit rates annually (13% in 1987, for example), but new business is going mainly to newly-established and highly professionalized companies. And the middlemen are being squeezed.

Dutch insurance brokerage firms, for example, are in the process of shedding some 6,000 jobs. Increasing complexity of insurance services and rising competition in this sector in the light of the integration of the European market by yearend 1992 help explain why the 8,500 insurance brokerage firms in the Netherlands must face up to a major restructuring. The Dutch Association of Insurance Brokers expects that only 2,500 to 3,000 companies will survive by 1995.

The largest European life insurance group is Standard Life, based in Scotland. Financial services in Scotland have a total payroll of some 110,000, double the amount of employees that are left in coal, steel and shipbuilding. Even although the insurance industry may be in crisis elsewhere, the Scottish life insurance business created an additional 2,000 jobs in 1987 alone. Scotland is to focus its development strategies for the next few years on the "Europe of the Regions", planning to ally itself more directly with financial services companies from Catalonia, Bordeaux, Lyon, Denmark and Northern Italy.

French insurers are also gearing up for 1992 and beyond. The merger of Compagnie du Midi and Axa has created France's second-largest insurance group after Union des Assurances de Paris (UAP). Italy's Generali, Europe's largest personal insurer, holds 20.9% of Midi. UAP has also created links with Sun Life of the United Kingdom. Meanwhile, Groupe Victoire, a Suez associate, has been negotiating with the Royal Group of the United Kingdom. And the French re-insurance group Scor has taken control of Vittoria Ri, the leading Italian insurer.

In Italy, there are 1,100 banks. In Spain there are more than 500 insurance companies. And Belgium has another 300 insurers. Huge disparities in the financial services market structure throughout Europe explain differences in cost to the consumer. The Bureau of the European Consumer Unions has calculated that the average life insurance premium costs about ten times more in Portugal and up to three times more in France and West Germany than in the United Kingdom.

American Express has proposed a telemarketing operation to sell insurance through a joint venture with an established insurer on the basis of its 2.8 million European cardholders: the cost is as little as ECU 180 per contract.

Several leading banks understand this very well. So-called "Bancassurance operations" are multiplying. The example above in the Netherlands is only one. French banks now write more than 50% of new life business. Predica, the life insurance subsidiary of Credit Agricole was created as recently as 1987 but is already now one of France's top three life insurers. In Germany, Dresdner Bank has concluded an alliance with Europe's biggest insurer Allianz. German banks will probably more than double their 15% share of life and pension market over the next five years.

If other banking, insurance and distributors do not move soon and with vision, these three major traditional services may well emerge as the 21st century equivalent of the steel and shipbuilding industries.

CHAPTER SEVEN

Anatomy of the New Services

In this chapter we take a closer look at some examples of the "new services" which have made an increasing impact on the world business environment. Since it is not practical in the present context to go into detail on every new service, we have opted for a representative selection, ranging from ostensibly mundane services - such as cleaning and maintenance - to leading-edge categories, such as database services and telecommunications.

Who are the key players on the market? What makes them special? What makes them tick? What makes them capable of double-digit growth?

1. Cleaning and Maintenance

The world market for cleaning and maintenance is estimated at between ECU 15 and 20 billion. It is a fast growing sector of a rediscovered service industry. Thousands of cleaning companies worldwide are poised on the threshold of internationalization. Inevitably, there will be a massive shake-out and countless takeovers as the leanest and fittest position themselves in a global marketplace. In Europe, there are more cleaners than bankers.

At present, countless employees in the cleaning industry are transitting from the "black economy circuit" towards formal employment, complete with social security protection, annual holidays, pension schemes and, not least, opportunities for further training and even a career. This is only possible on the basis of high productivity and increased professionalization.

The market for cleaning services is highly segmented, depending on the specific needs of each sector. The following market segments impose separate cleaning management techniques and have led to the establishment of independent subdivisions and even new companies specializing in these niche markets: general office buildings, hospitals, industrial buildings, hotels, supermarkets, private homes, laundries, schools, public transport, and computer equipment cleaning services.

Large cleaning companies are diversifying actively into multi-services for buildings. Those services include security services, energy saving services, building repairs, building supplies ranging from new doors to plumbing, complete carpet refurbishing and applied software for the cleaning and maintenance sector.

The largest cleaning company in the world - and, at the same time, one of the most diversified ones - is International Service Systems (ISS), the Danish-based services group with over 137,000 employees and fifty-three subsidiaries spread across fifteen countries on three continents. ISS has expanded dynamically on the European and U.S. markets by pursuing an aggressive acquisitions policy. The internationalization of ISS has brought the Danish group to Brazil and the  United States. Its president, Poul Andreassen, has probably done more for this "simple" sector than any other executive in the business.

In 1990, ISS had another successful year, with turnover in real terms progressing to ECU 1.1 billion. In addition to cleaning, ISS is active in laundry/linen service-development (vacuum cleaners) and in the sale of cleaning materials and machinery. It has also diversified into catering, security services, energy control and "intelligent buildings" management. Even with this impressive size, ISS controls less than 1% of the potential world market for cleaning services, with 2% of the German and American market, while topping 6% in the United Kingdom. ISS has designed a unique 5-star training programme for all its supervisors. Next time you leave your office late, you may meet a three or even a five star cleaning general!

The opening of new markets can also be exemplified through other successful companies. Service Master (Chicago, USA) has 80 hospitals under contract in Japan for cleaning services; Pritchard (United Kingdom and part of BET) cleans the International Hartsfield airport in Atlanta, Georgia; Pedus, the leading German cleaning group, sweeps office building floors in Budapest and hospitals in Italy; the Japanese cleaning group Tokyo Biso Kogyo has now opened subsidiaries in Taiwan, Singapore and Honolulu. DGS International, a part of the SGS group, performs major maintenance contracts in developing countries. The market has indeed become global.

The cleaning market is dominated by small and medium-sized companies. This can be illustrated by reference to some figures for the Belgian market. There, an estimated 54,000 people are employed in cleaning services, with almost 40% working for companies that declare less than ECU 100,000 in annual payroll. More than 50% of the Belgian workforce in this sector works for fewer than ten cleaning companies. The top five are all multinational groups of Dutch, Danish, French and North American origin.

The contract cleaning market for buildings in the Netherlands is valued at ECU 1.5 billion, of which 54% or ECU 0.8 billion is contracted out. There are an estimated 4,000 cleaning firms in Holland which employ approximately 120,000 persons. Office building cleaning contracts form the largest share of the cleaning market (62%), followed by hospitals (22%) and schools (16%). The level of concentration has progressed steadily over the years: 10% of cleaning companies now control 87% of the market. The five largest cleaning firms are Hodon (Vendex), Hago, Randstad, General Office Maintenance (GOM) and Asito. The Dutch subsidiary of the Danish group ISS is in sixth place.

General Office Maintenance (GOM), founded 25 years ago by Mr. J.G. Geurts, which is active in the Netherlands, Belgium, Luxembourg and France and which employs 10,000 persons in 30 outlets, has also set up its own electronics department to design and manufacture security systems (Teleguard). GOM has even succeeded in exporting to Japan its in-house-designed software for cleaning management; a translated version is used by Tokyo Biso Kogyo, an ECU 660 million turnover group employing 6,000 full-time personnel. ISS writes its own software through its data processing and information system company (ISS Data) which contributes to both management and the design of new products and services. Hodon developed the first professional fully robotized vacuum cleaner which is being tested now in its companies in Holland, Belgium and France.

Levels of productivity vary dramatically. Whereas a cleaning lady could competently handle fifty square metres an hour, today's leading companies can sweep floors, vacuum clean, dust, polish, wash windows and empty wastepaper baskets at the incredible speed of 400 square metres per hour. Given such differences in productivity, it is no surprise that cleaning services have become part of the formal economy. Moreover, it is understandable that the company which succeeds in attaining such levels of productivity will go international and offer its organizational knowhow abroad, using local personnel.

The potential for contract cleaning services represents a market of some ECU 13 billion in the EC. Among the factors that influence the demand are rising standards of living with related emphasis on quality of life, changes in methods of production (e.g. in relation to pollutive activities) and consumption (throwaway packaging), changes in occupational patterns (shifts from manual to white collar jobs), improvement in the quality of buildings and the ease of cleaning, improvements in cleaning technology, labour costs, and so on.

Even if total requirements of cleaning are expanding relatively slowly, demand for the services of general contract cleaning businesses has been growing, mainly due to increased contracting out of this service away from less productive in-house cleaning, i.e., cleaning done by directly recruited part-time or full-time labour. Currently, in the more advanced economies, companies and even public authorities in search of improved cost efficiency increasingly contract out their cleaning services to specialists.

Cleaning firms now account for over 40% of the total cleaning market in Belgium and France - compared with 25% in 1970 - with widely ranging percentages for the various market segments. In France, contract cleaning covers 82% of the market for large retailers, two-thirds of real estate, transportation, financial establishments and food industries, and about half of the hospitals. Of total demand, about half is accounted for by commercial and administrative premises. In the United Kingdom, private contractors cover something like 20 to 30% of the total market.

The major clients of the cleaning contractors are public authorities at all levels, which use contract cleaning firms for their buildings and equipment such as schools and universities, hospitals, airports, museums and cultural centres, railway coaches, etc. Other important customers are industrial, commercial and service companies. The British Institute of Cleaning Science has estimated that, in the United Kingdom, roughly one-third of the total demand for cleaning comes from the private sector and two-thirds from the public sector. Private contractors are estimated to cover over half of the private market but a much smaller proportion of the public sector market. The situation has been changing over the last few years as the U.K. Government has obliged the public authorities to put out to tender cleaning and related activities such as refuse collection, ground maintenance and laundering (e.g. in hospitals). In Belgium, public authorities of various kinds represent about 40% of the contract cleaning market.

Most part-time workers are female: over 90% in the United Kingdom, 75% in Germany and Italy, and 70% in Belgium. In France, 60% of the employees are female. In some countries, there is a tendency for the number of male workers to increase, in particular for night work and specialized assignments (e.g. refuse collection). Cleaning services employ some 60% of foreign workers in France and about 40% in Belgium; in the Netherlands this figure is close to 10%.

Contract cleaning is a dynamic service industry which can be expected to continue to grow rapidly.

2. Security Services

Security services are a profession with broad scope and multiple specialization, servicing a fast growing market. Rising crime rates, increasing wealth, spreading vandalism and terrorism and the ever greater complexity and vulnerability of modern societies have continuously expanded the demand for security services. Concurrently, the widening use of computers to record, store, analyze and transmit data has given rise to growing concerns about the security of data. Within the security services sector itself, modernization has been progressing, moving from the simple installation of locks and safes to the provision of sophisticated services involving advanced electronics and "intelligent" security devices. Notwithstanding all this, manned services for guard patrolling and transporting valuables as well as bodyguards for the protection of persons, remain characteristic of this activity. It is still a relatively labor intensive service sector, highly dependent on the quality and integrity of the personnel.

Overall, the security services market in Western Europe (excluding the manufacturing activity of security equipment), exceeded ECU 7 billion in 1990, with total employment of about a third of a million people and some 5,000 companies of all sizes. Manned guard services and intruder alarm systems each represent somewhat less than a third of the market. Annual growth of this service industry is in the order of approximately 10%. It is stimulated by constraints on manpower in the public sector and by a sharp rise in the demand for protection against terrorism, notably at airports, sporting events and exhibitions.

At present, the U.K. financial sector is spending some ECU 122 million annually on data security equipment and services; this figure is expected to reach ECU 227 million annually by 1992.

The U.S. market for private security services is estimated at ECU 20 billion, whereas the government budget for local, state and federal police services is only ECU 12 billion. One million persons were employed in private security services in the United States by the late 1980s, and the Department for Labor reported an additional 200,000 jobs created in this sector by 1990.

In the United States, there are one third more private security employees than policemen. This phenomenon is not confined to the United States: security services in Japan are also growing at an unprecedented pace. Despite the fact that, by international standards, Japan can be considered a safe country, the number of security personnel (170,000) has outstripped the number of policemen (100,000). Obviously, security service companies do not offer the same services as policemen do. It is rather an indication of how the overall market is evolving.

Two Japanese companies have secured market leadership - Sogo Security and Secom. Neither even existed thirty years ago.

ADT is the largest electronic security services company in the world. This company, which is also specialized in car auctioning, supplies professional services to over 250,000 businesses and homes through a network of over 140 central stations of which over 100 are in the USA. After decades of impressive growth, ADT registered its first downturn in 1990.

The European market leader is Group 4 Securitas, the Hague-based group, which had a global turnover of ECU 480 million in 1990. Group 4 Securitas is active in security services in Western Europe and the United States. Group 4 Securitas, dynamically led by Jørgen Philip-Sørensen, employs some 10,000 people, has 28,000 clients and specializes in security installations and equipment such as high security alarms, access control systems and closed-circuit TV systems. The sale and servicing of security-related technological equipment accounts for over one-fifth of the company's revenue. Group 4 Securitas controls about one quarter of the Swedish security services market through its sister Securitas, remarkably well managed by Melker Schörling. One of its fastest-growing new subsidiaries is its venture in India.

The fastest-growing security services group in the Arab world is Security Holding, based in Tunis. This group of six companies was founded in 1976 by Bechir Ben Amor. He employs today over 5,000 persons and is expanding rapidly throughout the region, with major contracts in the Middle East. Security Holding has set up the High Institute for Industrial Security to train guards. Diversification into electronic security systems started in 1987. This Tunisian group has taken over numerous contracts in Africa and the Middle East which were considered hardship posts for Western companies. Security Holding can offer the service at one third of the cost and its employees not only speak French, English and Arabic, they often have been trained in Western Europe as well.

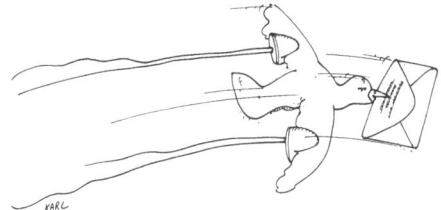

3. Courier Services

Courier services provide worldwide on-demand delivery of time-sensitive documents such as cheques and other financial papers, tender offers, blueprints, shipping and engineering documents, legal papers, etc. The express service also transports urgent dutiable items such as samples, circuit boards and other equipment, spare parts, periodicals, news media, etc. This service greatly facilitates the close coordination of activities in widely separate geographical locations, especially with respect to banking, trade, transport, and professional services.

Since the early 1980s, courier and express delivery services have been growing by leaps and bounds. With their integrated facilities, the major companies operating in this area provide worldwide rapid, reliable and carefully monitored door-to-door transportation.

Today, the main players on world markets - and also the most dynamic ones - such as DHL and Federal Express, operate worldwide networks and generally own their own airlines and fleets of vans and even telecom facilities. Their customers have recourse to them to obtain express, secure and efficient delivery. On-demand collection, rapid tracing of the shipments, and unified administrative control from end to end are their typical features.

Originally used to forward documents, the services of these companies are now gradually being used also for freight, notably because more companies are shipping their goods in single items rather than in bulk as part of a strategy to cut their inventories. Express and courier specialists have sufficient control over their individual door-to-door shipments to be able to offer reliable "just in time" delivery. High tech companies such as computer manufacturers have been among the first to use express services as a means of distribution. Their products are high in value, yet low in weight and easily transportable. Fashion retailers also benefit as it allows them to avoid stocks that can easily become obsolete. Innovative services to respond to new types of demand are on the rise, such as warehousing and inventory management on behalf of transnational manufacturers near transport hubs. This enables express companies to help manage stocks of parts and materials in the most efficient way.

Most of the revenues earned by the operators is spent locally, on personnel (one third), on transport (one quarter) and on administrative overheads (telephone, advertising, administration). The present size of the U.S. market (several hundred million pieces) shows that there is plenty of growth potential in Western Europe for this dynamic service industry.

DHL Worldwide Express is the market leader in Europe. It started in 1969 as a courier of shipping documents between Honolulu and the West Coast of the USA. DHL has more than 1,397 offices in 186 countries, serving nearly 70,000 towns and cities, all linked by state-of-the art technology. It employs some 23,700 people worldwide and transports about 60 million documents and packages a year with *inter alia* a fleet of more than one hundred aircraft and some 8,000 vehicles. Its main centres are located in Brussels, Bahrain, Hong Kong, San Francisco, Toronto, and Singapore. In 1990, DHL posted a record turnover of ECU 1.6 billion. DHL systematically makes use of advanced computer and telecommunications technologies to run its network and constantly track its shipments.

Table 7.1.   10 leading Express Courier companies in Europe

DHL International
Elan Services
Emery Worldwide Services
EMS (Postal Services)
Federal Express
IML Air Services Group
Jet Services
Overseas Courier Services
TNT Express Worldwide
UPS

Source: author

Express courier services first focused on the transportation of documents, then small parcels. More recently, the mailing service has evolved into a range of complementary communications services extending from traditional courier services through small parcel services, high quality fax, telex networks and remailing to express forwarding of heavy freight.

The evolution of the worldwide express industry has been influenced by regulatory laws which were originally designed to accommodate industries predating the express services sector. Such regulations include national postal monopoly laws, international postal treaties, national customs laws, and national and international transport laws.

The future growth of the industry will depend on the degree to which these laws can be adapted to the unique characteristics of the express services business and, in particular, on the extent to which national legislation can be harmonized to permit consistent international operations.

The world market for courier services was estimated in 1990 at ECU 11.3 billion, growing at 16% yearly. The U.S. market is not as buoyant as it used to be, but markets are expanding dramatically in Europe, in the Far East and in Australasia.

The annual turnover of domestic courier service companies in the United States *(intra US traffic)* is estimated at ECU 7.5 billion; this compares with ECU 28 billion for the Postal Service. Federal Express is the leader, with a 39 % market share. Fred Smith has spearheaded this service and brought it to a level of respectability few could have imagined a decade ago.

U.S. courier companies handle 650 million items per year. This is a marginal market share compared with the U.S. Post Office - which handles between 500 and 600 million letters and packages a day - but nevertheless a lucrative one. In order to face up to this new competition, the U.S. postal administration has of late been investing between ECU 240 and 400 million annually on improving its optical character readers, machines designed by AEG of Germany, which can handle 33,000 items an hour, or ten per second.

In the European Community, total *cross-border* express shipments in 1989 were estimated at 21.3 million pieces, handled by a workforce of over 75,000 people with a turnover of ECU 1 billion. The perspectives for growth in the European market are phenomenal. Further rationalisation can be expected in the 1990s, with the largest part of the business becoming concentrated in the hands of a few, large, global companies that are expanding rapidly, notably on the basis of active acquisition and shared participation policies.

The market has been growing between 20% and 50% annually, with the fastest growth noted in Spain, Greece and Portugal, and the slowest in Germany. It is perhaps no coincidence that Germany has the most rigid postal administration.

In the United Kingdom alone, there are over 1,000 domestic courier services and 125 international services. Meanwhile, DHL is now present in more countries (186) than Coca Cola and Marlboro, although the company only started to internationalize its operations in 1979.

Paolo Vittadini started Pony Express in Italy in 1984 and employs today 10,000 motorbike *aficionados* as part-timers. Some 200 similar companies have since sprung up across the length and breadth of Italy.

Door-to-door small parcel delivery is the fastest-growing diversification trend within Japanese trucking companies. In Japan, 194 small parcel delivery companies handled together one billion parcels in fiscal 1990 (ending March

1991), 4.8 times more than the Japanese Post Office.

The market leader here is Yamato Transport, which controls 40% of the market. Other contenders are Fukuyama Transporting, Seino Transportation and Nippon Express. Nippon Express is Japan's largest integrated transport company with a turnover of ECU 7 billion. Yamato Transport employs 37,410 persons and has a turnover of ECU 2 billion. Last year, Yamato income grew by 16 % and net profits fell 30% to ECU 17 million. The company maintains 1,165 delivery centres throughout Japan. Yamato has now branched out into house removals and transporting skis, surfboards and golf clubs for the increasingly large leisure market: Yamato picks your golf clubs up at your door and guarantees that they will be waiting for you on arrival at the clubhouse.

The world freight transportation market is a traditional service where innovation has created new profit centres. The parcel mail network is one example where entrepreneurship has led to improved competition and a faster and cheaper service to clients.

State monopolies feel the pinch - and react. National postal systems have decided to launch their competitive service on this growing market which had nibbled away a profitable share of their traditional business.

Express Mail Services is the generic name for the joint venture of twelve post offices in North America and Western Europe. EMS was set up in 1987 and carries different names throughout Europe: Chronopost in France, Datapost in the United Kingdom, and so on. The company benefits from the existing network of post offices around the world and from its excellent links with customs authorities. EMS documents and parcels are transported throughout Europe on DHL planes. More than 100 postal administrations are linked into the system and more are signing up, including the USSR. TNT secures the international links for the Postal services of Germany, France, the Netherlands, Sweden and Canada through GP Net, a first public-private partnership in this field.

Growth in courier services in Europe is forecast to continue at between 20 to 50% annually for several more years, depending on the country. The market for parcels will grow even faster than the documents market. Traffic in Western Europe is some 70% intra-European and is expected to become even more so with the completion of the European market in 1992.

At first, courier service companies were selling time. As time is money, documents that could be brought to a destination faster represented cash in the bank. Today, courier services have integrated into the just-in-time management philosophy applied by both manufacturing and distribution companies: courier companies arrange for delivery and storage of goods so that they arrive at the place where required "just in time" in order to save on inventory and storage costs.

Courier services depend heavily on their service infrastructure. They all have car fleets, their own radio channels and their own regional distribution hub. Courier consignments collected in each country are sent to a central point from where they are sorted and forwarded.

Brussels is now established as the leading express courier hub in Europe. It is a unique example where the then Minister of Transport, Herman De Croo acted with great vision and pursued this unique opportunity with an entrepreneurial drive all too few politicians display. Six of the top ten courier companies in the world use Brussels Airport as the focal point for their overnight operations: DHL, Fedex, TNT, Skypak, Pandalink and EMS. The DHL hub in Brussels handles three times more planes every night than the cash-strapped national carrier SABENA. Emery International has chosen Maastricht in the Netherlands as its hub, and UPS and Elan International have set up theirs in Cologne. DHL uses Budapest as its hub for Eastern Europe.

Express courier service companies have transformed themselves into heavy investors in private communications networks as they seek to keep track of each consignment which is being delivered around the world. All major operators use automatic call distributors to accelerate incoming telephone calls. Central computers allow them to pinpoint the location of every package from the time of pick-up through each of seven intermediary steps prior to the point of delivery. Portable optical bar code trackers, designed by the service companies themselves, relay the data via optical signals to the central computer and networked data terminals and delivery vans.

All leading courier service companies offer remailing services whereby clients classify the mail in two bags: Europe and non-Europe. The client pays the courier company a fixed price per kilo and the courier firms send the bags to the country of their choice from where regular postage will guarantee the fastest and best quality regular postal service.

TNT and DHL have meanwhile become the two single largest customers of the Belgian Post Office since they opted to centralize their remailing activities in Brussels. In other words, the lines of competition and cooperation between public and private services are becoming blurred.

The market for courier services is booming. At the same time, however, it is hampered by a plethora of rules and regulations. The most important problems faced by this sector in the wake of liberalization of the market are a streamlining of customs services; 24-hour traffic for parcels and envelopes and their clearance at airports; and harmonization of VAT and indirect taxes. In several countries, the courier service companies have to circumvent existing government obstacles in a "creative" way.

In Italy, for example, courier services are only permitted if the courier service firm affixes stamps to the parcels at the ongoing rate as if they had been sent by regular mail.

4. Language Management Services

Language services include translation, which is a major segment of the market, interpretation and language teaching by private institutions and firms.

The world market for language services has been estimated in 1990 at some ECU 18 billion and is growing at between 15 and 20% per year. This growth will continue, bearing in mind - for example - that only 13% of all software produced in the United States is currently translated and only 10% of Japanese scientific publications are translated into English. The American Senate has passed the Japanese Technical Literature Act which provides special funding for the training of Americans in Japanese and research into state-of-the art machine translation equipment in order to improve access to the massive pool of commercial and technical information available for free in Japan - albeit in Japanese.

The populations of Belgium, Luxembourg, the Netherlands, Sweden and Switzerland are multilingual. It is scarcely surprising, therefore, that these countries have positioned themselves rapidly on the world market for language-related services.

Belgium has a special advantage in that its capital, Brussels, plays host to an estimated 6,000 professional translators, the largest concentration in the world, outpacing by far both London and Tokyo. The European Community requires all official documents to be translated into the nine EC languages, a time-consuming and costly task carried out by over 1,000 in-house translators. In addition, the Community and its constituent institutions hold over 8,000 meetings per year, each of which requires on average 15 or 16 interpreters. This translates as 115,000 interpreting days at ECU 300 to 410 ECU per day. By comparison, the United Nations operates in five official languages and NATO, the North Atlantic Treaty Organization, in only two.

80% of the market for translations derives from bluechip companies in the high-tech end of industry - computer sciences, electronics, biotechnology. To provide such clients with consistently high quality service, language groups also invest heavily in automated translation research and development and in language databanks. INK, is a market leader with head office based in The Netherlands. Machine translation, an admixture of linguistics and computer science, is as yet primarily the concern of international organizations, public agencies and large transnational companies.

A market niche for language services is found in the translation/dubbing of motion picture soundtracks. Mexico generates an estimated ECU 120 million annually via dubbing of English movies into Spanish. FilmNet, part of the Swedish Esselte Entertainment Group and with 24,000 employees, translates approximately 450 English films per year into French, Dutch, Swedish, Danish, and Finnish at an annual cost of approximately ECU 2 million. The translation of each film takes one week. The translation is then transferred to the soundtrack through the pulsing of a floppy disk, making for perfect synchronization.

Demand for interpretation has grown along with the demand for translation-interpreting and for the same reasons. However, in this segment of language services, market expansion was also stimulated by the spread of simultaneous interpretation in the 1960s. The emergence of this technique made possible the multiplication of international meetings with, as a result, a booming demand for conference interpreters.

Of the 2,000 members from 65 countries of the International Association of Conference Interpreters, some 1,200 reside in the Community and 420 in EFTA countries (350 in Switzerland). About one fourth of these 1,200 Community interpreters are permanently employed by international organisations, the rest are free-lance and thus more likely to be rendering services upon request all over the world. The EC is thus very probably a substantial net provider of interpretation services to the outside world.

There are hardly any studies that assess in business terms the teaching of foreign languages in Europe. The Economist Intelligence Unit, however, recently conducted such a study on the teaching of English. The study reveals that, in the United Kingdom, the selling of English courses to foreign visitors is estimated to earn Britain about ECU 800 million a year and is thus its sixth largest invisible export. If the sale of books, the earning of teachers abroad and other revenues are added, the market could, according to the study, be worth around ECU 1.4 billion. These sums of course cover much more than the fees for the lectures and include expenditure by foreigners on accommodation, living etc. Still, with about 500,000 people coming to the United Kingdom to take advantage of its 700 or so language schools, the British market is quite sizeable. It is expected to continue to grow at a rate of at least 10 % a year, with competition from other Western European countries intensifying.

The above figure would tend to indicate that language teaching is a fast growing service industry in the Community, running to several billion ECU.

EF language school founded in Lund, Sweden by Bertil Hull, has 40 offices worldwide on four continents. It employs 6,500 people, including some in France, the United Kingdom, Spain and Germany. Among its language courses it has developed "linguistic holidays." EF Headquarters moved from Lund via Lucerne to Boston, USA. EF has positioned itself as the number one in "language travel". EF was, for example, the Official Language School of the Seoul Olympics.

Berlitz, based in Princeton USA, is part of the Macmillan publishing group (taken over by Robert Maxwell) and has 275 schools in the world, of which 160 are in Europe. It employs 3,000 people and averages 100,000 students daily, about half of which are European and one quarter American. Berlitz International publishes pocket travel guides and phrase books as well as offering commercial translation services and language tuition.

Linguarama Ltd, an international group with headquarters in London, provides language courses in over forty schools spread over eleven countries, including seven EC Member States. Overseas establishments are in Japan, Brazil and the USA.

Elsevier Languages, the language institute of the Dutch Elsevier Training Company, is expanding its network of language schools beyond the Netherlands, notably to Belgium (through acquisition), soon to be followed by Luxembourg and France. It also produces and sells software programmes for learning languages. Club Med includes language teaching in its holiday programmes.

Demand is growing fast in the Community. This is confirmed by a recent survey by Peat Marwick McLintock of the pharmaceutical, defence and aerospace industries in the United Kingdom that found that two fifths of the companies covered were considering recruiting European language specialists in readiness for the completion of the Single European Market.

Language services have close ties to advertising, marketing and communications, publishing, printing, desk-top publishing, electronic mail, franchising, temporary employment, software development and databank services. As a result, language strategies have become an integral part of overall marketing strategy, as experience with international airlines shows.

Trans-Pacific passenger traffic is increasing at the rate of some 15% annually. The key to capturing a share of this travel market is to have flexible and well-distributed access to reservation systems. All Nippon Airways, Japan Airlines's competitor, has reached agreement with Sabre, the computer systems operation of American Airlines. United Airlines has linked Japan's largest travel agencies into its Apollo network to permit on-line reservation with 650 airlines and more than 17,000 hotels. All systems operate in English only.

The U.S. computer specialist group Bolt Beranek & Newman has signed an ECU 23 million contract with JAL to integrate the latter's internal computer systems and to instal a translation system which permits flight reservations to be recorded simultaneously in Japanese and English. This should result in head-on competition with existing U.S. reservation systems. Over the next few years, JAL will invest ECU 200 million per year to instal computers, develop software and train its staff in a bid to compete more effectively against U.S. airlines which have captured over one third of JAL's market share since their computer systems were put in place. Language-related services have been singled out as a key tool for competitiveness. You have to talk the language of your client.

The productivity of translation/language management companies has shown impressive growth. And contract sizes have expanded accordingly. Contracts to translate one million pages in three to four months are perhaps still the exception, but they are increasingly common. After all, the introduction of new car models on the European market requires hundreds of thousands of pages of manuals. The computer industry faces the same problem. Each new computer needs manuals, perfectly translated into the local language. IBM has opted to subcontract the manual writing: a full time external team works on the premises of IBM Netherlands to get the job done. Being a translator is not enough: you need to be a computer expert and a linguist. In other words, multidisciplinary.

5. Fast Consumer Services

New consumer services are frequently developed in response to a vital corporate or consumer need: to save time.

Kwik-Fit Holdings is the largest independent car tyre and exhaust replacement company in Europe operating out of over 600 individual centres with more than 450 centres in Great Britain and a further 150 principally in Holland, Belgium and Ireland. The Company provides a fast-fit service with the highest commitment to customer service achieved through highly motivated and well trained employees of which there are more than 3,500. As well as tyres, exhausts and shock absorbers, brake repair and car safety products such as the fitting of safety belts and child seats are important new lines of business. Kwit-Fit continues to expand and, in the year to February 1991, sales were 19% higher at ECU 329 million and pre-tax profits were 62% higher at ECU 35.2 million. The founder of Kwik-Fit, Tom Farmer, started this success story when he was merely 28. He has maintained double - digit growth from year one.

Minit's worldwide network serves 25 countries on four continents. Minit owns and operates service centres and, 1990, had served over 60 million customers. Minit offers fast solutions to its customers through shoe repair and cutlery sharpening services, key duplication, a range of personalized printing and graphics services, photo development, watch repair, and sewing and clothing repair services. All services are offered from outlets in high-density traffic locations, most on a while-you-wait basis. By the end of 1990, Minit International boasted some 4,700 service centres throughout the world, with a total turnover of half a billion ECU. Surprisingly, Minit International is the market leader in Japan. It is not that the Japanese are incapable of copying a key. It is simply another proof of how even simple services can evolve into organizational technologies.

Minit International was founded by Dr. H. Ryan in 1957 and the company has enjoyed double - digit growth worldwide ever since. In 1989, Minit International was awarded the title "Europe's most performing service company" for its remarkable achievements. A privately held company, it does not disclose details of its operations. It is nevertheless a remarkable success to be able to set up small shops which generate between ECU 500 and 1,000 per working day focusing exclusively on fast consumer services.

6. International Moving Services

The world market for moving services was estimated at 12 billion ECU in 1990. The American market is the largest one in the world, with an estimated turnover of ECU 3.6 billion per year for 1989. Each year, an estimated 14.4 million American families change homes. This generates a demand for a variety of services. The moving market can be sub-divided into two major segments : domestic relocation and international moving.

54 % of all families that change homes in the United States move under their own steam i.e. they do not have recourse to specialty services. 28% of the total are "self-movers", renting equipment, whereas only 18% call upon a professional company to assist their relocation. However, this 18% represents 67% of the total turnover of the American domestic moving service industries. The remaining 33% is the turnover in the sector generated by rental equipment.

Since 1980, the American market for moving services has been largely deregulated. As the result of a fierce price war, there emerged a new market structure. The top ten carriers in the USA today control 85% of the U.S. market. One of the largest companies in the world is the North American Van Lines, headquartered at Fort Wayne, Indiana. North American Van Lines has 2,000 employees and operates through a domestic network of 800 agents.

U.S. moving services handled in 1988 approximately 150,000 international relocations. The large bulk of those moves involved the relocation of executives of leading multinational companies. The most important destinations are the member states of the EC. In view of the American response to the 1992 Single European Market, the increased mobility of European executives within Europe and the multitude of recent European and Japanese investments in the USA due to a lower dollar, international moving services are expecting double digit - growth over the next five years.

The moving business outside the USA has been dominated by a multitude of small and medium-sized companies. But, due to a recent trend towards mergers and acquisitions, larger concerns are emerging which will be in a position to provide a much broader service across the globe. The British market leader Pickfords Group recently acquired Allied Van Lines, the second largest carrier in the United States. The largest Japanese moving companies are Nippon Express and Yamato Transport.

The leading companies in the moving services sector have diversified extensively into related businesses. North American Van Lines started specializing nearly 15 years ago in the distribution of high value added products and electronic equipment such as computers and photocopiers. North American Vans also developed a distribution network for "white products" such as refrigerators, dishwashers and washing machines. The largest mover in Benelux, Arthur Pierre

Table 7-2. **Market leaders for international removal services**

Amertrans	UK
Atlas Van Lines	USA
Arthur Pierre International	B/FR
Crown Pacific	Hong Kong
Fink	Brasil
Graebel	USA
Interconex	USA
Interdean	Germany
Klingenberg	Germany
North American Van Lines	USA
Pélichet	Switzerland
Pickfords Removals	UK
Trans Euro	UK

Source: author

International, has also diversified into distribution under the brand name Pulsar, and into export crating of goods under the name Quasar Industrial Export Packing Services. The holding company Arthur Pierre International controls branches in Paris, Lyon, London, Rotterdam and Luxembourg. The group employs 350 people, has over 100 trucks and operates 8 warehouses. Arthur Pierre plans to open new branches in the majority of EC member countries in the light of the integration of the European market by 1992. 90% of Arthur Pierre's business is international.

New technologies are changing the face of the removals business. In the USA, the major van lines have developed a computerized monitoring system for the thousands of moves they handle yearly. Unfortunately, the lack of internationally compatible computer standards has meant that no uniform global system has been developed up till now. Under the aegis of Arthur Pierre, a multi-million ECU deal was negotiated with a software group and a hardware supplier to have an integrated computerized monitoring system operational for Europe. This system is now fully operational and links all major Arthur Pierre branches.

New transport techniques have also facilitated higher quality and security of moving services. In the past, removals were packed in wooden liftvans; today, goods are transported in containers, and air-ride trucks offer a more comfortable ride for the furniture, and, since recently in Japan, for the family (which can install itself alongside the furniture in a comfortable container). Packing as such has converted itself into a specialized technique for increased protection of high quality household goods.

The increased mobility of business executives consecutive upon the globalization of activity in the free market economies and the ever expanding corps of diplomats and international civil servants has been accompanied by a rising demand for international removal services. The continuation of this trend will ensure double - digit growth for the sector for a number of years to come. In Western Europe, the run-up to the Single European Market in 1993 is spurring change not only in the internal structure of companies but also in the inward and outward movement of direct investments, thus guaranteeing a steady rise in the movement of people.

7. Conference and Exhibition Services

The increase in the number and the size of meetings, and rising expectations as regards quality and efficiency have over the years given rise to organizational, administrative and management techniques which require professionalism. Amateurs and improvisers have largely had to give way to meetings managers who have built up their credentials and become competent in a truly professional sense.

The task of conference organizers consists in the setting up of the detailed programme, establishing the budget, selecting the meeting premises and ancillary facilities, supervising hotel and food arrangements for the participants, recruiting interpreters, promoting the event with likely participants through advertising, mailing, etc. and, finally, running the administration of the conference. Like so many other activities, this service is now moving fast towards a global market. Conference organization techniques have become increasingly standardized and sophisticated and ever cheaper transportation has broadened the choice of locations. Europe's still remarkable eminence in the market for international conferences is slowly eroding.

Product presentation conferences for the launch and/or demonstration of new products such as fashion or car models is a segment of the corporate meeting market which has grown along with the other marketing tools. Incentive conferencing (including travel) is a modern marketing and personnel management tool to stimulate employees' performance; it has now expanded beyond the sales and marketing area where it started to extend to many categories of employees and workers. It is of recent appearance on the market, at least in its present dimension, but as part of the policy of corporations to invest in human resources it has been growing by leaps and bounds.

A remarkable new feature of today's multifaceted "corporate market" is the booming number of meetings that are convened by publishers such as Elsevier, the Financial Times, l'Expansion, the International Herald Tribune and The Economist which programme conferences on selected topics in various cities of the developed world. These publishers have overtaken traditional trainers and seminar organizers such as Management Centre Europe. To these institutions this activity brings public relations benefits and a source of information and contacts for their journalists. One of the pioneers in Western Europe was the European Management Forum (now the World Economic Forum) which started in the early 1960s with its annual Davos symposium and which now also conducts annual conferences in a dozen countries. Davos is a *big* money maker. Next to the demand originating from the business world, there is the international conference market created by the demand from intergovernmental organizations (IGOs) and that from international associations/organizations. IGOs now number around 500, including those belonging to the U.N. family. As most IGOs are located in Western Europe (the main exception being the U.N. New York headquarters) and many of them in the EC (London, Paris, Brussels, Rome), it follows that Western Europe benefits greatly from this economically profitable segment of the market.

The trend towards greater mobility is even more marked with INGOs (international non-governmental organizations). Such organizations number in the thousands (at least 6,000) and are still multiplying. As almost all these INGO's are located in capital cities (the exception in Europe being Geneva), the Community is again well placed to benefit.

At the world level, the "national and international conference market" has been estimated by American sources at some ECU 60 billion with annual growth rates of some 8 to 10 %. This would correspond to some ECU 20 billion for Western Europe. According to the same U.S. sources in the U.S., attendance in 1987 at about one million off-premise meetings by some 74 million people constituted a record.

The international conference market has experienced impressive and almost continuous growth over the last three decades, reaching close to 8,400 meetings in 1988. Growth in 1990 is expected to top 20%. 43% of these meetings were held in the Community, 11% in the USA. The latter figure is in no way representative of the dimension of the U.S. meeting market because the geographical size of the United States turns into national meetings what would, in most other countries, be international meetings.

Over the last fifteen years or so, Western Europe's share (today still around 50%) as well as that of North America (15%) have gradually declined, to the benefit primarily of East and South Asia. Member States of the Community figure prominently amongst the leading host countries.

Paris, London and Brussels were respectively numbers one, two and three in a top ten list for international meetings compiled in 1990, and Europe is certainly the focal point for world conference activity. Out of the ten most popular conference venue cities, only two are non-European - New York and Singapore. For the record, the other cities most in demand are Geneva, Vienna, Berlin, Rome and Strasbourg. Conferences are a labour-intensive services sector, with flexible working hours. They also represent major export earnings potential.

A study conducted in 1987 by Italcongressi concluded that in 1986 the conference business in Italy had contributed some 0.8 % to gross national product. This figure includes direct expenditure of the participants and the people accompanying them (some ECU 2.5 billion) and the outlays of the organizers (ECU 115 million) multiplied by a factor of between 1.6 and 1.8 to adjust for indirect effects. The same study estimated that sector employment, both direct and indirect, during the same year was 95,000, with 65,000 in jobs directly, but not always exclusively related to the conference business.

Every day, there are an estimated 100 to 200 conferences, seminars and workshops held in London - a staggering 20,000 or so meetings annually. As noted earlier, France already generates more foreign exchange from conferences and trade fairs organized in Paris, Marseille, Nice and Lyon than from its automotive exports.

Not surprisingly, investments in conference facilities are booming around the world as organizers battle for a share of this explosive conference and exhibitions market.

A study of the volume and structure of the German meetings market in 1987 reported a total of over 150,000 meetings with more than 50 participants generating some ECU 1.6 billion in revenue in terms of conference facilities and hotel accommodation. To this are to be added secondary earnings, i.e., expenditures by the roughly 17 million participants on travel, shopping, personal needs and so on. Dutch figures on the international conference market in the Netherlands in 1988 report 140 international conferences with a foreign participation of 47,000.

The pace of economic growth does not seem to influence so much the demand for conferences, whether national or international, as it does the number of participants. Intergovernmental conferences, not surprisingly, are basically recession proof.

There is no easy way to ascertain the amount of employment generated by the conference sector. Together with the temporary staff to which most organizers have recourse, the "equivalent full time" jobs relating to the conference organization business in the Community may well run around to one hundred thousand. But the largest employment creation aspects of the meeting business lie in all the support services for participants such as accommodation, catering, transportation and the many other conference ancillary services described above. In these activities, the jobs run into hundreds of thousands. Typical of this service industry is the high participation of females.

Whereas the conference business in the USA is a mature service and fully competitive, Japan although number one in Asia, still lags behind. Today, Tokyo is Japan's leading conference city with about one third of all international meetings. Hong Kong, Singapore and Kuala Lumpur have both invested heavily in recent years in conference and exhibition facilities to attract international conventions, especially in an attempt to lure American and Japanese businessmen to their cities.

Germany is the European leader in exhibition services, with some 30% of international business. The Hanover Fair, the Frankfurt Book Fair and the Textile Fair draw visitors from the whole world to Germany. The United Kingdom now has a 10% share of this sector. German companies earmark on average 25% of their public relations/public affairs budgets for exhibition activity, whereas U.K. enterprises spend approximately 10% on exhibitions, up from 3% only a few years ago. The total budget of U.K. companies in 1990 was estimated at over ECU 400 million, while total spending on exhibitions, including foreign spending, was close on ECU 700 million. *Fortune 500* companies each spend on average ECU 1.6 million on a major exhibition.

Blenheim Exhibitions, the fast-growing British exhibitions organizer affiliated with the French holding Lyonnaise des Eaux, has followed the acquisition trail both in the United Kingdom and on the Continent since it came to the U.K. Unlisted Securities Market in the mid-1980s. Blenheim organizes exhibitions for a wide range of industries from fashion to computer technology and arts and crafts. Spectrum Communications and Peter Rand Conference Placements are Blenheim's principal U.K. competitors.

8. Personnel Services:
Executive search, outplacement, selection and recruitement

The world market of some 1,600 executive search firms is estimated at around ECU 3 billion. The U.S. market alone amounts to ECU 2.3 billion with 1200 offices and the ten biggest firms taking one third of that market. The top ten headhunters in the United States doubled their turnover between 1984 and 1988. In 1987, revenues generated by overseas assignments were for the first time higher than the fees obtained for U.S. assignments. The leading ten firms report a 141% growth in billings for international searches over the past three years, whereas the growth in US billings was only 64%. The top four companies account for 10% of all billings.

The world market leaders in the headhunting game are Korn/Ferry and Russell Reynolds. Europe's market leader is Switzerland-based Egon Zehnder International, which is also in third spot worldwide, with an annual turnover of some ECU 70 million. Egon Zehnder is rapidly closing the gap with the market leaders. Peat Marwick was the first autonomous executive search company division to be set up by one of the "Big Six" accountancy firms: PM generates ECU 21.6 million in fees worldwide. To date, only three accountancy firms have diversified into executive search consultancy.

Executive search is a segment of the broader recruitment services sector in which consultancies identify people that correspond to the profile of a post to be filled and then personally ask them if they would be interested before proposing them to their clients. Such search services based on a personal approach differ from those of selection consultants who advertise jobs and then pare down the entries to a short-list for the client employer. Search consultancies as a rule only offer their services for upper or middle level posts. They are best suited to cases where the skills and experience needed to do the work well are possessed by only few readily identifiable persons.

Some consultancies specialise horizontally by sector (informatics, finance, pharmaceutical industry), others concentrate on a vertical segment according to the level of the job (top or middle management). Executive search is a highly competitive market, which thrives particularly in unstable economic conditions. Economic crisis/boom conditions are best for the industry since they tend to lead to changes in personnel requirements, both in terms of numbers and in terms of requisite skills.

The leading consultancies which run their own set-ups are Korn/Ferry, Egon Zehnder, Spencer Stuart, Russell Reynolds, and Heidrick and Struggles. Linked networks with other consultancies are Canny Bowen, TASA, and Ward Howell. Boyden International has opted for the structure of cross-ownership.

The fees obtained are a percentage of the first-year salary of the person appointed, although some charge according to the difficulty of the assignment and the time needed to succeed. The large consultancies reduce their number of clients and form a more in-depth relation. The drive for more billings has led in the last few years to an invasion of European companies purchasing American search consultancies.

Executive search consultants are diversifying into related businesses in an effort to maintain growth. Heidrick & Struggles purchased Eurosurvey, a market research company; Egon Zehnder offers temporary executives and management consultancy advice; Spencer Stuart has set up a joint venture for corporate turnaround services; Whitehead Mann, the fifth largest British search group has segmented its organization accordingly to the market, i.e., search for start-ups and fast-growing small companies, a management audit and assessment service and a selection company for lower-level assignments.

Several executive search companies have focused their business within well-defined niches. Robert Half and Accountemps have combined recruitment of accountants from two different angles, depending on whether the client needs permanent or temporary staff. Robert Half and Accountemps have 120 networking offices around the world and are the market leader in this area of specialization. Japan Recruitment specializes in the selection of Japanese speaking personnel at all levels.

Several consultancies have emerged which supply specialized services to the executive search companies and their clients. Executive Compensation Service (Belgium) makes a regular calculation of the pay offered to management at different levels in different branches. ECS gives gross basic salaries, the buying power of the cash after deductions for tax and social security, and adjustments for living costs have been made. ECS also offers surveys on management rewards throughout Europe. Runzheimer International, a U.S.-based consultancy and PE-Inbucon (UK) offer an overview of yearly expatriate costs.

In Germany, this service activity is technically illegal, as it is in principle reserved to the national employment agency. However, in April 1991, the EC Court of Justice ruled that Member States may not reserve search activities for executives and managers to monopoly institutions. A double digit growth in executive search is now expected in Europe's largest economy.

There are an estimated 55 outplacement offices operating throughout Europe. Some assist management on a case-by-case basis, others have specialized in finding new jobs for an entire workforce because of bankruptcy or company closure. The outplacement offices generate their income from the enterprise which is firing the person. Sanders and Sidney, a U.K. employment counselling group specialized in outplacement, nearly tripled its annual profits in the year ending March 1991. It has a network of five regional offices in the United Kingdom and plans to become increasingly international. On the other hand, executives sometimes employ professional managers such as Executive Management International Ltd (UK) to advance their career interests and retain career development services for outplacement.

There are an estimated 500 recruitment agencies in Europe specialized in freelance personnel contracting. Computer programmers, systems analysts and designers are often needed for a single project. Changes in technology and the increasing importance of information management have created demands for new skills for a only a short period of time. A contractor earns through a recruitment agency 50 to 100% more than under a regular employment contract. The agencies take between 15 and 30% commission on the weekly fee.

Temporary Employment Businesses

The market for personnel related services is booming, diversifying, professionalizing and in flux. There are in Europe an estimated one million temps working each day. This means that the temporary employment agencies have approximately six million Europeans on file for potential temporary placement.

Even though few executive search and outplacement bureaux have diversified into "temps", the borderline between the business is evaporating. Indeed, Egon Zehnder offers temporary top management and GREGG, the leading temp agency in Belgium, does the same.

The essential characteristic of this service is that temporary employment agencies (TEAs) hire temporary workers and put them at the disposal of a third party to do temporary work for that party (the user). It is the TEA which assumes the normal role of employer for the workers concerned. Such a triangular relationship distinguishes interim work from limited duration work contracts or from casual labour which operates in a strictly bilateral worker-employer framework.

Originally, such temporary work services developed in the context of an overall labour shortage with the TEAs helping to bring "hidden" manpower into the labour market. It was mainly, if not exclusively, used as a stopgap to replace absent workers, to cope with a momentary extra workload or specialist task or to respond to a temporary activity not justifying the recruitment of permanent staff. It also provided jobs for those who did not seek to enter the permanent manpower market. Indeed, some workers are in no position to take on permanent work because they are only temporarily available; others prefer temporary work for the freedom and diversity which it offers.

On the user's side, recourse to TEAs has been increasingly motivated by a desire to obtain qualified personnel immediately, when such workers cannot quickly be found or when permanent use for such workers is not yet assured. User firms which resort to temporary labour and end up recruiting permanent workers thereby benefit from the personnel selection process used by the TEAs, which specialize in searching, interviewing and selecting temporary workers.

Over the last few years the temporary employment market in Western Europe (excluding Italy and Greece where this activity is strictly forbidden and Spain where it is tolerated in practice) has been rising at an average annual rate of 15 to 20%. In 1989, growth slowed to 10 to 15 %. For 1990, the value of the world market is estimated to have reached over ECU 31 billion. Turnover in the European Community is somewhat less than ECU 15 billion for the same year and the USA was contributing ECU 13.2 billion. In Europe, approximately one third of the market share is taken up by internationally-oriented groups.

Because temporary employment only plays a complementary role on labour markets, the numbers of temporary workers occupied on average each day still represent only around 0.5 to 2 % of the active population in those Member States of the Community where this type of work has developed, and only 0.6 % in the Community as a whole.

The ageing of the workforce in Europe, the increase in the female component of the working population and the increasing demand for temporary help in specialized areas (medical, data processing, accounting, catering) combine with a greater desire for more flexible work arrangements to augur well for further growth in the market.

With only 1% of U.S. employees at present working on a temporary basis, as against 2.5% in the United Kingdom, for example, or 2% in the Netherlands, U.S. growth potential in this sector is clearly enormous. The fastest-growing U.S. segment is that which covers health service-related employees.

The activities of TEAs have recently been growing strongly both in terms of number of local establishments created by temporary work firms and in terms of workers on assignment. The multiplication of local establishments provides a better service to client firms and facilitates the local recruitment of temporary workers. It is estimated that, in the Netherlands, more than 70% of all businesses use temporary help every year on a more or less regular basis. In France, the market for temporary workers has increased by 20% annually over the last three years. The activities of TEAs fluctuate. Both extremes of recessionary climate and full employment tend to reduce their turnover, which seems to develop best in a climate of moderate or brisk economic growth. The level of activity of TEAs is a kind of barometer for economic activity in general. Some EC Member States (such as the Netherlands) use it as a parameter, amongst others, to forecast the business cycle.

Manpower, the American multinational TEA with subsidiaries all over the world, is the largest "temp" business in the world with establishments in more than 30 countries worldwide (including Japan). The second largest in the world is Adia, a Swiss-based group with subsidiaries in all EC Member States. In 1990, the Adia Group's consolidated revenues increased by 3%, attaining ECU 2.3 billion. In the temporary help and personnel services sector, Adia's revenues rose to ECU 1.8 billion. The third largest TEA in the world is the ECCO from France. In the Community, one third of the market is taken up by such internationally oriented groups. In early 1991, Manpower moved its headquarters from London to the United States, thereby ceding to Adia the number one spot in Europe.

Table 7-3. **Market leaders per country in the temporary employment sector (1990)**

			Market Share 1990
USA	1	Manpower	8.6%
	2	Kelly	7.6%
	3	Olsten	4.8%
	4	Adia	4.4%
	5	Personnel/Med Pool	3.8%
France	1	ECCO	17.7%
	2	BIS	16.5%
	3	Manpower	15.0%
	4	Adia	7.4%
	5	RMO	4.4%
UK	1	Manpower Group	9.0%
	2	Adia Group	6.0%
	3	Hestair Group (BET)	4.0%
	4	Reed	4.0%
	5	Accountancy Personnel (Hay's)	3.0%
Netherlands	1	Randstad Group	31.0%
	2	Vedior Group (Vendex)	15.0%
	3	Start	12.0%
	4	Adia Group	7.0%
	5	Werknet	4.0%
Switzerland	1	Adia	20.0%
	2	Manpower	18.3%
	3	Ideal Job & Ok	14.2%
	4	ECCO	5.0%
Germany	1	Adia	5.6%
	2	Rummler	4.7%
	3	DIS	4.0%
	4	Bindan	3.5%
	5	Randstad	3.0%
Japan	1	Temporary Center	10.0%
	2	Manpower	5.7%
	3	Tempstaff	4.9%
	4	Career Staff	2.9%
	5	Adia	1.5%

Source: Adia, 1991

The market for temporary employment services is synergistic with other new services: language services, security services, cleaning and maintenance are all services where employment extends beyond standard working hours and often entails short-term assignments where there is a need for quality. Predictably, employment agencies have diversified into security and contract cleaning services. The Dutch groups Randstad and Vendex (Vedior), through Hodon, Cemsto and Cemstobel, have been most successful in offering this trio of services. France's ECCO and Hestair (through BET of the United Kingdom) have followed the same route.

Concurrent with the trend towards diversification into related services, employment agencies see a growing trend towards specialization. The leading example is Computer People, the U.K.-based employment agency for computer specialists, which offers software engineers, programmers and teachers. Another U.K. example is Comac, an employment agency specializing in procuring temporary staff for the transportation and distribution sectors.

Vedior International, the Dutch services group with shares in GREGG and Tempo, offers "temps" of every conceivable kind - ranging from a surgeon to a designer or a marketing manager - and offers advice on long-term personnel planning.

Peter Lane Transport, one of the leading independently-owned freight groups, recently expanded its operations to include a personnel agency specializing exclusively in transport personnel. As several companies have a fluctuating need for management at all levels due to shifts in distribution contracts, personnel management can be optimized through recourse to a service for outsiders called "personnel leasing", a pool of highly qualified people who can assume responsibility for seeing through a particular project.

Thus, temporary employment agencies are increasingly characterized by both diversification *and* specialization.

The market for employment services is highly regulated. Denmark only permits temps in commerce and administrative services. Germany, the Netherlands and Belgium exclude temporary employment agencies from the building and construction market. The use of temps is not allowed to replace workers on strike in France, Belgium, Germany or the Netherlands. Contract duration is limited to three months in Germany and Denmark. There is a contract duration limit of six months in the Netherlands. Regulations are most flexible in the United Kingdom, Ireland and Luxembourg. In the latter two countries, temporary employment agencies have no specific status in law, the result being that the provisions of national labour law are applied.

In view of the demand for flexibility and fast access to qualified personnel, companies have specialized in sub-contracting labour whenever temps are forbidden. From the legal standpoint, there is little difference, although in sub-contracting it is the company offering the employee which is responsible for the management and supervision of his or her work. By contrast, temps are controlled and supervised by the client company. The most common system in countries where employment agencies are forbidden is simply to operate through the parallel economy.

Employment agencies are now more and more concerned to offer services which extend significantly beyond the original concept of tiding a company over a temporary situation. Increasingly, they are emerging as companies capable of offering integrated personnel management services ranging from clerical staff to computer specialists, high level technicians and even managers. As a result, temporary employment agencies are heavy investors in databases, office networks and communications systems. The investment in computers and communications as a percentage of turnover is variously estimated at between 2 and 5%. Computer companies eager to sell their hardware and services have here one of their prime market segments.

9. Educational Services

Educational and training services offer firms and public enterprises a variety of professional, vocational, skill and quality enhancement lectures and programmes in management, leadership, human relations, sales and marketing, administration and finance and technology, particularly information technology. The overall objective is to help client firms and their personnel achieve greater organizational and individual efficiency and to raise levels of quality and performance. There are a small number of well-known training and education companies such as TMI (Denmark), Tom Peters (Europe, USA), and J. Juran (Hutchins Associates Ltd).

But this wide, diversified and not very precisely defined branch of business services does not seem to have ever been studied in depth and no comprehensive figures or estimates about its size and growth are available. What is clear, however, is that, in recent years, the supply of training services has been experiencing constant and vigorous growth. It is recognized that most people starting their careers today will have to change their profession or line of activity at least three times over their lifetime. Awareness of the urgent need in Central Europe and the Soviet Union for training in the skills and functioning of market economies has recently given an extra impulse to this services sector.

In Western Europe, larger enterprises and those with qualified personnel tend to devote more efforts and resources to professional and vocational training. Some public administrations also have intense recourse to outside professional teaching and training assistance. In France, the law provides that firms with ten or more employees must spend 1.1 % of their gross salary outlays on educational programmes. No such obligations would seem to exist in other countries of the European Community.

Each year, there are about one million foreign students worldwide following one-year courses.

The United States plays host to more than 340,000 students, over one-third of this total. Japan takes only 10,000 foreign students today, but has decided to increase its overseas student population tenfold, to reach a total of 100,000 by the end of the century.

In 1989, U.S. income from education services rendered to Asia, Africa and Australasia amounted to ECU 3.2 billion. The largest proportion of paying students comes from Asia: 22,500 from Taiwan, 21,700 from Malaysia, 16,400 from South Korea, 14,600 from India and 13,100 from Japan.

In 1989, there were an estimated 5 to 6 million students following short-term courses abroad. Of these courses, the most common were those devoted to language training, followed by sports and cooking. In this last-named market segment, Japan is the largest importer: young girls of good families are traditionally sent to cookery courses overseas prior to their marriage. Switzerland and France are the most important host countries for this specialized service. In 1989, there were 56,000 overseas students in the publicly-financed U.K. higher educational system. This represents nearly 10% of the total U.K. student population. Students came from a total of 177 countries (out of a total 204 countries), but over one third were from just four countries: Hong Kong, Malaysia, the United States and Nigeria. An estimated 284,000 overseas students were enrolled in an estimated 350 private colleges in 1989. Of these, 93% were following English-language courses.

Time Manager International (TMI) established by Claus Møller, the former personnel director of ISS, is the world's leading company specializing in the teaching of management, personal development, service productivity and quality. It has subsidiaries and licensees in more than 42 countries. TMI offers seminars, consultancy, planning tools, books and audiovisual systems whose overall objective is the development and improvement of people and organizations. TMI's so-called "change programme" is applied throughout the company concerned, and aims at raising productivity, improving interpersonal relations, developing quality and helping to cope with change.

Since TMI was established in 1975, almost two million people have taken part in its training programmes. Several thousand large and small organisations in the private and public sectors have benefitted from its assistance and improved their work methods. The "change programme" has been adapted to companies such as SAS, British Airways, Japan Air Lines, Telecom New Zealand and the Commission of the EC and has received wide recognition. In recent years, Central Europe has become a major growth market for TMI. By the end of 1990, it had trained over 12,000 Soviet officials and managers. TMI employs 500 people and has a turnover of close to ECU 50 million.

10. Consultancy

Figures on the value of the "management consultancy market" are extremely difficult to compile.
They are sensitive to definition and at best, merely
well-informed guesses. The German Management
Association (BDU) recently produced figures for
the value of management consultancy throughout
Western Europe for 1989. It estimates that close to
17,000 management consultancies, employing
some 122,000 consultants, earned gross revenue
of roughly ECU 16 billion.

Others take wider definitions however, and believe that the market may be nearly
twice as large. The biggest segment of the market (some ECU 15 billion) includes
education and training, software development and maintenance, while another
segment general management consultancy may be worth more than ECU 4
billion.

Whatever, the market for management consultancy is simply huge. Government
and public enterprises and institutions such as state utilities, hospitals and
educational facilities have themselves significantly contributed to the demand
for consultancy, particularly those specializing in computer services. Many
consultancies now obtain more than a third of their work from public contracts.
Some countries, such as the United Kingdom, even subsidize the use of
consultants by small firms.

Overall, the demand for general consultancy work is anticipated to continue to
expand at well over 10 % per year, while continued higher growth can be forecast
in the segments of information/communication technology. Indeed, these days
a computer installation is necessary for just about any project - even in human
resources. The need for global computer solutions remains enormous. In terms
of expected growth, management/organization followed by strategy consultancy
come next.

High double-digit real rates of growth in West European management consultancy were the hallmark of the golden years of the 1980s, particularly the second
half. Only recently has the service in certain countries, such as the United
Kingdom, for the first time experienced a downturn; this will probably turn out
to be only a brief period of consolidation.

Elsewhere, in France, Italy, Spain and Germany, annual growth rates up to 25 and
30 % were recorded until 1990.

Western consultancies have also rapidly been expanding in Eastern Europe to
respond to the needs of these economies characterized by extremely weak
service sectors and an almost total lack of modern management, marketing and

financial skills. In some countries such as Spain, Italy, Portugal, Greece and even certain market segments in France, consultancy remains at a relatively modest level, thus offering excellent prospects for vigorous expansion.

Spurred by this potential profitability, accounting firms and companies in other sectors (such as banks, law firms and advertising agencies) have been entering the management consultancy market. Mergers and acquisitions have multiplied as well as alliances between smaller consultancies. And, in turn, the management consultancies themselves have been moving into other activities more or less related to consultancy, such as public relations, communication, market research and legal advice.

Next to the accounting sector with its many firms that have crossed boundaries into general consultancy work, there are the companies that have continued to concentrate on their original management consultancy activities. Here again, several large groups, mostly *Anglo-American*, stand out.

Table 7-4.   Market leaders in consultancy services in Europe

Andersen Consulting	USA
Arthur D. Little	USA
Bain	UK
Berenschot	Netherlands
Roland Berger	Germany
(controlled by Deutsche Bank)	
Bossard	France
The Boston Consulting Group	USA
Booz Allen & Hamilton	USA
Kienbaum	Germany
KPMG	USA/Netherlands
McKinsey	USA

Source: author, 1991

These offer advisory services at the top level (strategic advice) and add to that specialized abilities such as personnel management, knowledge of retailing or finance, etc. They help identify management problems, analyze them and recommend solutions including, when requested, assistance in implementation. The European management consultancy sector offers good earnings prospects. In the United States management consulting revenues of the Big Six more than doubled to ECU 8 billion over a five-year period. This tendency will not be so strong in Europe, as the relationship between accountancy and management consultancy is still moot.

In some EC Member States (Belgium, France, Italy), government regulations require that auditors should not render non-auditing services to their clients, and the accountants are obliged to create separate legal entities to provide out consultancy services. There is no such barrier preventing software companies from entering the management consultancy sector. They will continue to seek opportunities for acquisition of consultancies (mainly SMEs), looking for new entries through strategic and production management. Other professions such as banks, law firms and advertising agencies continue to enter the consultancy sector for the same reasons. In 1989, Deutsche Bank acquired the leading German consultancy Roland Berger.

In 1990, most in demand were personnel management and training consultancy, where fee income increased by 85% in the United Kingdom alone. The second largest increase occurred in manufacturing management and technology, where fee income rose 60%. Fees from projects in information technology increased by only 33%, although they had doubled the year previously.

Companies engaged in market research are enjoying a boom.

Five out of the top ten market research companies in Europe posted a 20 %-plus growth in turnover in 1989, and eight out of ten recorded double-digit growth. Research revenue from consumer clients still represents 43 % of this growth, followed by media research (10 %) and advertising-related research (6 %). Market research in the financial sector soared 30 % but still only represents 4.5 % of the total market.

The accountancy service sector used to be dominated by accountants and statutory auditors who provided their services to clients, both individual and corporate, in the public and private sectors. Their services traditionally extended to tax advice and other related activities such as insolvency analysis and trustee work. However, for over a decade, the sector has moved from being financial advisers to becoming advisers in many other areas of business and government services. The large multidisciplinary accounting firms in particular have thus gradually branched out into all kinds of consultancy assignments such as management consultancy, corporate finance and information technology consultancy.

The best known are the so-called Big Six: KPMG, Ernst & Young, Arthur Andersen, Coopers & Lybrand, Price Waterhouse and the merged DRT (Deloitte, Ross, Tohmatsu). However, the cooperative formula between Deloitte and Touche only operates in the USA and some other countries, whereas in several Western European countries, the Deloitte consultancies have entered into arrangements with Coopers.

All these companies originally specialized in accounting services but have over the years turned into multidisciplinary consultancies. Today, they remain the world's biggest auditors with offices in numerous countries and some 130,000 staff in Western Europe. Apart from Arthur Andersen, which is highly centralized, and Price Waterhouse which is somewhat less so, the links between the practices in different countries of these conglomerates vary from common partnerships across borders to loose affiliations involving no profit-sharing arrangements. As these groups broadened their expertise and spread geographically, largely through mergers and acquisitions, in order to provide more comprehensive service to clients who had themselves branched out, their interest in general consulting activities, with higher profit margins, increased continuously to the point that in several of them earnings from consulting now exceed audit income. Amongst the recent high growth areas have been company valuation, and mergers and acquisitions investigations. In Western Europe, the fees obtained by the larger accounting consultancies have been growing at comfortable double-digit rates for several years.

KMPG is the world's leading firm of accountants, auditors and consultants. Created in January 1987 by the merger of Klynveld Main Goerdeler (KMG) and Peat Marwick International (PMI), it has 6,300 partners and 77,200 staff in more than 750 offices in 114 countries. Fee income for 1990 was ECU 4.7 billion. 67% of income is generated by traditional audit services, whereas consulting makes up 12% of the turnover, the remaining 21% being tax advice. Andersen Consulting, associated with Arthur Andersen, was the first consultancy linked with an audit company to generate over ECU 1 billion in consultancy fees.

Several new subsectors are emerging in the consultancy market. Industry is increasingly aware of the need to pursue an environmentally sound production system. Consultancy related to the environment is a key component of the diversification of existing advisory groups, but has also prompted the entry of new corporations on the market. SGS, the world market leader in quality control and inspection and ABB, the world's leading energy specialist with more than 240,000 employees, are vying for this future market. In view of their unique expertise, it will be difficult for the traditional houses to compete. There is an unprecedented erosion of boundaries.

Quality programmes constitute another important new segment for the market. No company can now afford to produce products or services without aiming at the best quality for a reasonable price. Quality improvement has become a vital prerequisite for any company. The International Organization for Standardization has set standards for quality of services summarized in the ISO 9000. Companies such as SGS (once more) and Philip Crosby Associates are proposing programmes to protect the customer and the supplier through quality programmes, implementing quality management systems. This is another new segment with a remarkable potential.

11. Design Services

Europe has the oldest traditions in the field of design. Its strength lies in the great diversity of national characteristics that allow it to prosper in a variety of styles such as "Italian design" or "Scandinavian" design and more simply "European Design". Design extends over a wide range of disciplines. Its expertise applies from physical modelling to publishing and TV graphics, from space planning to brand and company image.

At the global level, estimates from the industry for fee income from "commercial architecture and design" report a world market in 1989 of somewhat over ECU 27 billion, of which one half for the U.S. market and about one third for Western Europe.

In that overall total, "commercial architecture" represents two thirds, and interior design (including retail shop design) and product and graphic design (including corporate identity) each approximate to one sixth.

Europe has a clear lead in the world market for the expanding high value-added services. Whereas the U.S. and British markets have gone through a slowdown since early 1990, Continental Europe's design market has continued to grow apace.

Table 7.5	**Major design firms in Europe**
Belgium	Axel Enthoven (Industrial Design)
Italy	Pininfarina (Product Design)
	Italdesign (G. Giugiaro) (Industrial Design)
	Ghia (Industrial Design, owned by Ford)
	Bertone
Spain	Ricardo Bofill (Architectural Design)

Source: author, 1991

In the Community, Italy is the most important exporter of industrial design. Its four leaders have diversified into prototype building and engineering feasibility studies. Its product designers have found interesting clients in Japan and the newly industrializing countries of Asia.

The turnover in 1988 of Danish design services covering industrial/product design (but not engineering), graphic communication, and interior design (but not architecture) is estimated at some ECU 62.5 million, with two fifths each for industrial/product as graphic communication design and one fifth for interior design. The number of consultancies is estimated at 200 and total employment is about 1,000.

The United Kingdom stands out with its very strong presence on world markets for that part of the design market that is closely related to advertising/communications activities. British groups have been expanding forcefully by acquisitions and today of the top ten international design networks in that segment of the design market, all except one (Landor) are British or, at least, British owned. They are WPP (design division), Addison Consultancy, Fitch-RS, Siegel & Gale (based in New York but owned by Saatchi and Saatchi), Pentagram, the Conran Design Group, Wolff Olins and Minale Tattersfield. Their branches or subsidiaries are spread all over Western Europe, North America, the Far East and Australia. Their design fee incomes in 1988 ranged from ECU 7 to 8 million. However, in 1990 several of these firms went through a period of painful adaptation and restructuring as their domestic market - the U.S.market - temporarily dried up.

In all EC Member States, the design business today is still very much at the cottage industry stage. A vast majority of the consultancies employ less than 5 or 6 people, are owned by the people that run them, and specialize in only very few disciplines. It is a service activity based more than most others on imagination, inspiration, talent and hunch rather than on standard parameters. Many professional specialists claim that the culture of a craft-based activity like design is not compatible with size as it inevitably leads to losses in creativity. They therefore keep their staff small.

Among the fastest growing sources of interior design work, there are the professions, the leisure industry and retailing. For graphic design, food and drink manufacturers and financial services score well. For the multidisciplinary consultancies, the same six sectors and, in addition computer and office equipment manufacturers, are excellent clients. Not surprisingly, there seems to be a correlation between the dynamism of individual economic sectors and recourse to design assistance. For example, computers and leisure score well amongst the rapid demand growth sectors. In industrial design, cars have been the stronghold of Community designers, mainly from Italy.

In some EC countries, as, for example, the United Kingdom, public authorities such as those in charge of health, employment and police are turning to "identity design" consultancies to advertise their services and improve their public image. The public services market has tremendous growth potential.

As one of the most dynamic sectors of the European economy, design consultancy has witnessed a high rate of business creation, particularly since the early 1980s. The profession is unrecognized and unregulated in most Member States.

Entry to the business is easy, with little need for significant capital investment. People are the key asset. A good part of new business is generated because of background factors like reputation, rather than through any direct marketing action. The most productive marketing technique seems to be to do good work for existing clients.

It is in graphic communication that some further specialized activities are to be found such as "annual report and brochure design" and the somewhat more esoteric "language simplification". The former is one of the success activities of Pentagram of London which has a major presence in this market not only in Western Europe but also in North America. Language simplification (which consists in rewriting needlessly complicated forms or legal texts in a clear, simply, more accessible way for tax forms, bank contracts, etc.) has found a leader in "Siegel and Gale", the main design subsidiary of Saatchi and Saatchi, the worldwide British advertising and marketing services group.

Corporate identity is also a relatively recent and fast growing discipline where U.S. and U.K. firms were pathfinders on world markets (including that of the Community) but have now been followed by several others. This segment embraces a wide process of image management, the selling of an idea. It no longer simply begins and ends with a logo but involves every aspect of the image of a company in its relations with the public and, increasingly, with its own employees. Corporate identity has become part of what is now known as "corporate culture". It is expanding rapidly in Western Europe. In its most extreme form, a full package corporate identity contract, e.g. for a supermarket chain, calls for a team of designers in a broad range of disciplines from architects and ergonomists to product and package designers. This demand has been fuelled by the spate of merger and buy-out activity of the last few years that has *inter alia* called for plenty of new company names and images. Landor Associates of San Francisco, recently bought up by Young & Rubicam of New York, is the world market leader.

Manufacturers and service providers of all kinds have progressively come to recognize the central role of design in their activity. As price competition turned out to be an increasingly fragile strategy for competitive advantage, better design - functional and aesthetic - became a crucial marketing tool to boost products, services and workplaces.

Apart from creativity, design is business and must help to obtain results. Before working out a visual recommendation, designers needs to know from their clients what the objectives are of the products or services concerned, what the distribution is and what consumers' habits are.

In modern advanced economies, design has earned a place alongside engineering and marketing as one of the decisive factors for the success of products. Contemporary design consultancy, with its variety of disciplines, is in reality a new service industry. It has enjoyed apparently effortless growth for about a dozen years and, except for the time being in the United States and the United Kingdom, it is still vigorously extending its scope and skills. Even if some large groups operate on the market, design has still not abandoned its cottage industry roots. It remains characterized by versatility and generally by an attitude which embraces change and looks for challenge.

As in many other relatively new and fast growing service sectors, the industry has difficulty in finding designers of calibre. Recruitment problems are particularly acute in the southern part of the Community where demand for design for advertising and marketing services has been exploding and where there is little established teaching capacity or few businesses to train young people.

In the Community, a number of design consultancies have embraced information technology. They widely use computers as an administrative aid and also increasingly as a creative design tool. The emergence of three-dimensional video image design has forced a fast adoption of the latest technologies. Applications are of particular importance in the security services sector where often live situations have to be simulated on screens. This is of special interest in training for rescue operations for oil platforms.

Design services are actively promoted in the United Kingdom. A slew of new initiatives are being developed and launched by the Department of Trade and Industry in conjunction with the U.K. Society of Industrial Artists and Designers. These initiatives include a design awareness advertising and direct mail campaign, and an ECU 20 million budget earmarked for elaboration of a design management quality standard.

In the new age of marketing which started in the early 1980s, companies large and small have begun to embrace design as a key competitive weapon. Design is being exploited more and more to generate competitive identity and distinctiveness for products of all kinds, and to create a corporate culture through interior and exterior conceptualization of headquarters.

From Tokyo to Detroit, from Milan to Munich, from London to Los Angeles, the familiar strategic pattern which emerged with respect to top-of-the-range products such as Rolex watches, Porsche cars and Herman Miller office furniture is now spreading like wildfire to the world of mass marketing. The Swatch watch from Switzerland, the Olivetti from Italy, Olympus cameras and Sony stereos from Japan, CDs from Philips, shavers from Braun, and the S.W.I.F.T. headquarters building in Belgium - all are examples of companies having realized that "design" is not just an afterthought.

Instead, these companies and others have recognized that design is central to a company's strategic objectives. And that design, a multidisciplinary skill *par excellence*, can play a vital catalytic role in developing a company's products, reinforcing its marketing strategy or shaping its corporate culture.

Today's designers are different. They have evolved away from the notorious individualists with outsize egos and quasi-"artistic" pretensions; today, they are more level-headed, more cooperative, more business-like.

Europe's designers do not all hail from Milan and other design-rich parts of Italy. Ettore Sotsass, Mario Bellini, Rodolfo Bonetto, Giorgetto Giugiaro are undoubtedly key international designers, but no more so than Spain's architect designer Riccardo Bofill, or Germany's Richard Sapper and Hartmut Esslinger. A number of Britons such as Kenneth Grange and Nick Butler have also hit the front in the design stakes, and Belgium's Axel Enthoven deserves a special mention. Above all, however, one should not forget the unsung heroes who operate inside global corporations such as BMW or Olivetti.

With a few exceptions - Niels Diffrient is one of the few that spring to mind - most great American designers are names from the past. "Design" has become just another fast-growing service sector - alongside several others - where Europe has the lead. What is more, Europe is well-placed to maintain and even expand that lead.

12. Computer-Related Services

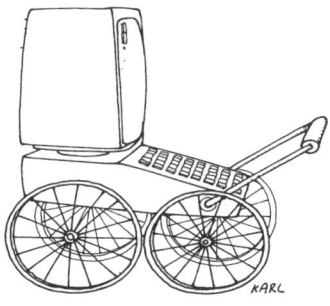

Dissemination of technology within a corporation is in response to user expectations. To increase their efficiency, users want new resources for acting on information: access to trillions of data, computer aided design and drafting, document handling, simulation, knowledge transfers and the like. The 40 million PCs installed in 1990 will be joined by at least 100 or 200 million before the end of the century.

Personal computers will then account for 75% of the installed base in contrast to 35% today. Can you imagine what an explosion of services is to be expected around this myriad of computer infrastructures?

Information technology is used in sales, finance, distribution, logistics, manufacturing and administration. It has changed the banking landscape, moving a substantial share of banking outdoors, sometimes even in the freezing cold. About three quarters of all cash withdrawals are now performed by automatic teller machines. Perhaps the most crucial segment of computer-related services is maintenance. After all, one breakdown is sufficient to keep your company out of the market ...forever.

The European market for computer maintenance is expected to top ECU 7.15 billion in 1990. The bulk of this market is held by the manufacturers themselves, with independent maintenance firms accounting for only 8% of the European market, or ECU 562 million. However, independent companies are gaining a strong foothold in the market, competing aggressively against manufacturers for lucrative contracts. Input, a market research firm, puts the growth of market share for independent maintenance firms at 20% annually in France, 22% in Italy, and 16% in Germany and the United Kingdom.

The maintenance cost for computers can vary between 3 and 15% of the hardware cost. The growth of computer networks which link personal computers and several larger systems on an international scale has improved the prospects of independent players in the computer maintenance market. Hewlett-Packard has begun to tender for maintenance contracts which include non-Hewlett Packard equipment. For Hewlett Packard, maintenance contracts account for ECU 850 million per year. NCR has decided to offer maintenance contracts for all computer systems. Open systems software seems to start in the real world with open systems maintenance.

There are an estimated 100 specialized computer maintenance service companies operating across national boundaries. Granada Computer Services, part of the Granada Group, is estimated to be one of the largest computer maintenance companies in Europe with a turnover of ECU 287 million (1990). Econocom, founded in France by Jean-Louis Bouchard, faced some difficult years, but now seems to have succeeded in streamlining its operations and is once more on the double digit growth track. In 1990, the group reported an ECU 400 million turnover.

Companies with large computer installations contract services out to a maintenance specialist company which keeps an engineer resident on site. The original manufacturers counter this strategy by offering all maintenance services themselves, also for different brands of computers. The manufacturers also deliver spare parts to third party maintenance companies so as to secure their market share. Granada Computer Services has had to turn away contracts because it sometimes cannot get access to the requisite spare parts. This protective strategy is considered illegal under the Treaty of Rome and will have to change shortly, offering additional growth opportunities to all players on the market.

Maintenance contracts require companies to respond to any call within four hours. If the engineer cannot effect a quick repair, the faulty computer will be replaced. Third party maintenance (TPM) companies have accumulated interesting data on the reliability of computers and peripherals. TPMs conclude that the largest number of defaults are with printers, and 20% are due to misuse by the operators - the most common cause in this category being coffee spilled on the keyboard.

Computer maintenance companies have accumulated very interesting first hand market data and have a direct view on which products and systems are most user friendly. Computer maintenance companies are starting to diversify increasingly into system integration. Recently, computer companies have become aware of this trend and have developed an aggressive strategy to recover lost market share.

13. Databank Services

The information services market in Europe will expand to an annual value of ECU 55 billion by 1992. By then, the Japanese market will be valued at ECU 24 billion and in the process of doubling again by 1997 to ECU 47 billion. The U.S. information services market will remain dominant in volume, peaking in 1992 at ECU 114 billion, up from ECU 52 billion in 1987.

The world market for databank consultations was estimated in 1990 at some ECU 9 billion and their growth has been calculated at 40 % per year. News databanks are to grow at a rate of 60 % a year. The United States runs an estimated surplus on their balance of trade of ECU 3 billion in information services, including videotext services, value added networks, electronic database services, custom research, and document supply services.

Today, there are some 6,000 internationally connected data banks available for public use. 95 % of the profits are generated by some 5 % of the companies active in this sector. The market is still very open for new initiatives. Minitel, the French PTT project, installed some 11 million terminals in homes, and over 10,000 databanks and services of all kinds have been connected, with growth rates peaking at some 3 % per month.

The databank market can be subdivided into a broad range of segments. Approximately 50% of the market is controlled by financial and economic information databanks many of which are updated each second. The other two major databank markets are the industrial databases, which are dominated by the patent and trademark electronic archives, and scientific databanks. Some infofiles are unique and cannot be classified under any other segment such as: AIDS, with 4,000 documents on the subject to which an estimated additional 2,000 are added each year.

Table 7-6.   **Market leaders in databank services**

Dialog	UK
Datastar	UK
ECHO	F
Patolis	J
Quick	J
Quotron	USA
Reuters	UK
Telerate	USA

Source: author

99

Over the years 1990-1992, some 1,000 new internationally accessible databanks will become available. This growth is good for a 28% increase in supply. Entry barriers to the market is relatively low and competition may come from unexpected quarters. American Airlines, for example, is the second largest databank supplier in the USA. Demand is the most important parameter in the databank market. There are an estimated 2 million regular databank users in the USA, whereas the total figure for Europe are tentatively calculated at some 150,000.

This tremendous growth in the supply of databank services has led to the creation of a new profession: the information broker. If you wish to know the value of a piece of art you contact (for example) ISK from Wiesbaden, Germany. This information broker has access to Artquest, a databank containing the prices paid for 810,000 paintings, drawings and sculptures in the leading British auction houses. Each year Artquest adds another 80,000 items. ISK is also connected with RILA, a French databank with an international repertoire of literature on art. The cost for one consultation will vary between 50 and 100 ECU.

The German government has decided to stimulate the development and professionalization of the information broker. The government has already approved support schemes for 135 new brokers, of which 64 are private companies, the remainder being public authorities, schools, universities, and research institutes. The German government subsidizes a part of their investments in computers, telecommunication equipment and in the translation of German databanks and on-line services into English, a precondition for internationalization.

In order to be able to consult a databank, one needs to master the special databank language to get access to the information. There are approximately 60 different databank languages on the market, of which some 20 are the most common ones. Several companies have arranged for a unique interface language. This permits the client to know only one language, which is each time translated into the databank's one. The client of Maxwell Online with 250 databanks under direct control does not even need to have a subscription to the different databanks. The interactive network language will automatically select the databank which will provide the information needed.

The on-line database can be updated continuously. Databanks can also be stored on CD-ROMs (compact discs with read-only memory) with a capacity of 200,000 pages on one 12 cm wide disc, equal to the information on 100 floppy discs. Today, CD-ROM represents only 7% of the total information market, but it is expected to grow at double digit rates in the next ten years. The world's largest supplier of CD-ROM is Maxwell Communications from the United Kingdom. The largest databank in the world for scientific and technical information is Patolis, the Japanese databank founded in 1955 with today 16 million patent information files. The first databank in the field of science was established in 1950 in the USA, a compilation of patents in chemistry. Each day there are 17,000 new scientific and technical publications. Without databanks, no one would ever be in a position to know what information is available and where. The market for databanks knows no frontiers: scientists from the USSR, Hungary, Bulgaria and Czechoslovakia have direct access to Western databanks though a node established in Austria by the Austrian Radio (Radaus). 50% of Eastern European demands are for American, 30% for West German and 20% for Swiss databanks. This node also permits Western scientists to call up Soviet scientific and technological information databanks, like VINITI with 46 databases, MCTVI with 6 databases; the chemistry and thermodynamics databank IVTAN, and three social sciences databanks (INION). Bulgaria has put its medical databank CINTI on the network.

Financial information databank services have been booming for over a decade. Glen Renfrew, in the ten years that he was chief executive of Reuters, charted a growth with revenues increasing from ECU 125 million in 1981 to ECU 1.9 billion in 1990 and profits increasing tenfold over the same period to ECU 446 million. Top executives and strategists like Mr. Renfrew have shaped this market for years to come.

Over the past four years, Reuters has doubled the number of its installed screens from over 100,000 to well over 200,000. Reuters reports real time from 164 money markets, and has nearly 1,000 journalists around the world together with some 4,000 correspondents. The company has 10,000 employees, remaining stable in numbers the last few years while profit and turnover keep progressing - perhaps the best proof increased value added for clients. Reuters generates 64% of its turnover in Europe where it maintains a healthy 20%+ growth rate, whereas America is only responsible for 16% and sales expansion has been greatly reduced. There, Telerate leads the way. Citicorp has teamed up with Quotron to emerge as a formidable player. In Asia, Reuters generates some 20% of its turnover, but sales are stagnant as well. The expansionist drive of Quick is certainly felt there more than anywhere else.

Financial information and news in all its forms is the driving force of the databank sector. Reuters is positioning itself further as the world's leading supplier of electronic financial services. In recent years, it has acquired Rich (1985), the U.S.-based designer and supplier of communication systems for financial dealing systems; Instinet (1987), a U.S. company providing electronic stock dealing service; Finsbury Data Services (1986), a U.K. firm selling full text retrieval services; covering business and financial information; and IP Sharp, from Toronto, Canada, a major computing services company. IP Sharp has a worldwide interactive data communications network. It is interesting to note that Reuters classifies itself as an electronic publisher and not as a databank.

We are indeed talking about a sector which is rapidly changing and the label given can very well change over the next few years. It seems that Reuters (financial information), VISA (credit cards) and S.W.I.F.T. (interbank telecommunications) will see their markets converge over the next few years rather than decades.

The need for more than just market power and access to technologies in services was clarified when IBM and Merrill Lynch decided to abandon Imnet. As Imnet was conceived, investors and brokers would have used IBM PCs to draw on a wide range of financial services. This appeared to be a potent combination. But Reuters, Telerate and Quotron proved to have a better grasp of the information needs of their clients and were able to achieve an organizational economy of scale which even blue chip companies like IBM and Merrill Lynch could not develop at a competitive cost.

The largest financial information vendor in Japan is Quick, 40% owned by the Nihon Keizai Shimbun, and a consortium of companies which includes most of Japan's leading brokers and banks. Market information from the Tokyo Stock Exchange and the six regional Japanese stock exchanges is channelled at 48,000 bits per second (bps) into Quick's computers. There it is massaged into tables and forms and then sent to some 40,000 terminals installed in stockbroker offices in Japan and abroad.

Quick is upgrading and internationalizing its services. Its terminals provide real-time information on stock prices, the Nikkei 225 average updated every minute and news headlines, information on bonds, foreign exchange and interest rates. Quick offers services in English as well as Japanese to 32 cities in 13 countries. Quick and Hitachi (one of its shareholders) are developing dealing room systems; dealing room systems happen to be one of Reuter's main products.

The third-largest provider of Japanese financial database services is Nomura Securities, also a shareholder in Quick. Nomura Securities has teamed up with Nintendo, the manufacturer of the phenomenally successful video game Famicon, and hopes that it can tap into the latter's vast user base.

The credit rating databases are one of the largest segments of the market, valued at over ECU 1 billion. The three market leaders are TRW, Equifax and Dun & Bradstreet. Legal databases are worth more than a quarter of a million ECU. Industry-specific databases in fields like computers and office equipment, pharmaceuticals, or investment goods are worth hundreds of millions of ECU each. Dataquest in computers, Nielsen (a division of Dun & Bradstreet) and SAMI/Burke (a division of Control Data) are the market leaders, though several companies are still vying for leadership.

A key sub-sector of the database market and one which is emerging with growth rates of more than 40% per annum is database update, maintenance and management services. Several companies view this as the most promising segment of the database market in the coming decade. And, in the Caribbean, a number of islands off the beaten track are staking their economic future on this simple but crucial service. Creativity - and the will to succeed - are enough.

14. Electronic Publishing

Companies without any connection to the printing industry are installing editing and typesetting equipment in their offices. The most important reason for those investments is gaining time. A document which would have taken three months to produce with an outside printer could take less than a week with an in-house electronic publishing system. A second reason is that electronic publishing in-house virtually eliminates the danger of information leaks.

Low cost computer equipment has opened up the world of publishing. Growth in electronic publishing is exploding at 60% a year. The market for electronic publishing catapulted from nowhere to ECU 900 million, considered to be 3% of the potential market. By 1991, the market will top ECU 4 billion.

Bertelsmann is the most surprising publishing group in the world. Led by Mark Wössner, the group has doubled its turnover from 1986/87 to 1989/90 from ECU 3.2 to 6.5 billion. Its average growth rate has been 18 % per year for over a decade. From traditional publishing Bertelsmann is moving into electronic media links through satellite TV, compact discs and data storage. For Bertelsmann, the U.S. market was a prime target: now it is focusing its energy on Eastern Europe. Bertelsmann has already acquired a 41% interest in Népszabadság, the leading Hungarian daily. Together with Maxwell, it has also bought Berliner Verlag.

The book club market, a form of direct distribution of books, has been turned into a pan-European business through Bertelsmann and Group de la Cité. Bertelsmann has 14 million book club members outside the German speaking market, including 5.4 million in the United Kingdom and 5.1 million in France as well as 700,000 in Italy. The production of books is not difficult: sales and distribution are key ingredients of success. Here, Bertelsmann has changed the face of the market.

Nowadays, information needs are being satisfied by a widening variety of electronic media and communication devices. Current developments in the printing industry indicate a close link between the printing sector and global developments in communication and information technology. Cross fertilization and mutual dependence are apparent in technology and in media usage. Competition between different market categories has been mainly directed towards increasing capacities.

Electronic communication should not be seen as something which does not concern printing services or which is *per se* directed against them. Apart from pure printing products and pure non-printing products, in certain parts of the information market there will be an increasing amount of "mixed information" i.e., purpose and user-oriented mixed solutions consisting of printed and electronic communication. This explains the efforts of the printing industry to open new markets in both areas by early participation in new information technologies and active diversification of business activities.

The electronic publishing market has been invaded by companies with the most diverse backgrounds. The market for electronic publishing has a low barrier of entry. Computer firms are entering manual production, advertising, language services, consultancy. Competition can come both from the back room of a student at university or from a major consultancy or audit outfit.

Today, anyone with the equivalent of ECU 3,000 or even less can purchase a personal computer, some special software and a laser printer; overnight, they are in the electronic publishing business. Auditors, anxious to exploit in book form their intellectual expertise in matters of taxation and accounting, are launching into electronic publishing. Deloitte, Haskins and Sells generates an estimated ECU 2 million a year with its desk top publishing unit.

15. Software Services

The world market for software and software services amounts to approximately ECU 115 billion. The U.S. market accounts for about 47% of the total, and the EC market for some 36%. U.S. firms are very strongly export-oriented, particularly in the area of standard software packages (Lotus 1-2-3, word processing systems, CAD systems, operating systems, etc.).

Marketing of this U.S. software in Europe mostly occurs via special branches of U.S. firms or via independent software suppliers acting as licensees. Both U.S. and European software and computer programming companies experienced tremendous growth between 1980 and 1990, with an increase of 500% in the number of establishments.

There are approximately 25,000 software companies in the United States. The largest in the world, Computer Associates has about 2% of the world market. Computer Associates has now merged with Uccel of Dallas to form the largest software house in the world. Previously, Computer Associates had already acquired other software companies such as Sorcim, Kapex, Johnson Systems and Issco.

The increase in the number of salaried employees in the software and computer programming sector in the United States was estimated at close to 600,000 in 1987. Since then, the increase has been some one hundred thousand jobs per year, passing the 1 million mark in 1990. The average age of a software developer is estimated at 24. The need for broad experience is next to nil: creativity and understanding the client's business are the two preconditions for success.

A conservative estimate reveals that, in the United States, there are some 60,000 software packages on the shelves. The three largest packaged software companies are Ashton-Tate, Lotus and Microsoft. The three companies started operations in 1982. Bill Gates, the founder of Microsoft has become the undisputed strategist of the packaged software market.

It is surprising that there are no genuinely trustworthy statistics on software services in Europe. That said, the three major subdivisions in software - packaged, custom-designed and systems software - each represent ECU one billion-plus. The EC market in 1989 for *software and software services* reached a value of ECU 29 billion. A market volume of approximately ECU 38 billion is forecast for 1992.

The total EC-market for *software products* (ECU 13.5 billion) can be divided into standard software, with total European turnover of about ECU 7.1 billion and customer-designed software worth about ECU 6.4 billion. Overall, the standardized software market in Europe is strongly dominated by U.S. imports. Europe imports some three million pieces of standard software per year.

Total EC *production* of software products (standard and customer-specific software, excluding related services) as a whole, amounts to ECU 10.1 billion and represents about 27% of world production.

The five largest hardware suppliers combined make more than ECU 10 billion from software worldwide. As software and services are growing at twice the rate of hardware, manufacturers have no choice but to take this route in future.

The trend has clearly proceeded in the direction of standard software. This is due to the fact that standard software packages are becoming more powerful, more flexible and better adapted to individual conditions. In addition, prices for standard software fall with growth in the number of units sold, so that its use is becoming increasingly attractive in terms of cost.

Differentiation of software products according to how close the software is to the system, indicates that software close to the system (operating system, programming languages, etc.), constitutes about 24 % of software products. The manufacturers of independent operating systems such as MS-DOS and UNIX are in the forefront of this movement.

In fact, Europe has proven to be a leader in customized software services. The undisputed pioneer is Mr. Serge Kampf who launched his business in 1974 and operates out of Grenoble (France). 60% of Cap Gemini Sogeti's turnover is generated outside France, 12% in the United States. Cap Gemini is by far the largest company quoted on France's second-tier market, with a market capitalization of more than ECU 1.8 billion in 1991. With a staff of nearly 19,000 employees, Cap-Gemini-Sogeti recorded a turnover of ECU 1.4 billion and a net income of ECU 93 million. The company increased its total work force by 40% in one year, gained a leadership position in the UK, doubled its presence in Germany thanks to the acquisition of SCS, and added facilities management to its range of services. Cap Gemini Sogeti surprised the world announcing its alliance with Daimler Benz, Europe's largest industrial group. Industry and services are once more twinning for growth.

On average, the twelve member states derive 0.38% of GNP from software development. These figures represent only the sales of specialized companies and do not take account of internal developments at the level of individual companies themselves. Estimates suggest that these internal developments have a market value equal to the total market volume.

In Asia, of course, Japan is the market leader, with an estimated 2,200 companies in the software and computer programming sector.

ASCII is Japan's most successful software supplier. In effect, the meteoric rise of ASCII Corporation over the past ten years is unique - even by Japanese standards. The founder, Kazuhiko Nishi, had all the odds apparently stacked against him when he started his company at the tender age of 21. Originally, the company concentrated on publishing computer magazines: it now has eight titles, each selling 500,000 or so per issue. But ASCII is better-known to the information technology fraternity as a leading software developer.

India and the USSR have the highest absolute number of software engineers and mathematicians. One can expect a major entry into the market by companies from these two countries over the next decade. Although the Soviets have not yet demonstrated a capacity to market their potential, Indian software engineers have already made a name. Recently, several software houses from the United States and Europe have decided to set up branches in India in an effort to overcome the high cost and the shortage of qualified staff.

By 1990, India was generating some ECU 450 million in software exports. India's main asset as a would-be software power is its labour pool of technicians - nearly 2.5 million English-speaking university graduates and 1.5 million software engineers - the largest pool of specialists in the world!

The second largest pool is in the USSR. With over 800,000 PhD graduates in mathematics, the USSR has an enormous potential which could be put to use in the Western computing and software services sector, where there is an acute shortage of qualified staff. It goes without saying that this manpower would be available at very competitive prices. In a very buoyant market, it is unlikely that we will hear early allegations of 'software dumping' brought against India or the USSR within the framework of the GATT...

16. Telecommunications Services

Telecommunications equipment suppliers expect the largest share of their growth over the next decade to stem from telecom *services*. CIT Research, the London consultancy firm, predicts that, by 1995, some 85% of the telecom market will be services. The total Western European market will grow to ECU 200 billion by 1995, up from ECU 105 billion in 1987.

Within the next twenty years, telecommunications services will emerge as the single most important economic activity in the European Community, outpacing the car and oil industry. Today, telecommunications represent 2% of Community GNP; by the year 2000, this will have grown to 7%.

The overall Western European telecommunications market will double in seven years time. Alternative network services such as mobile phones, cable networks, satellite communications and value added services such as information and electronic mail will grow from ECU 2.1 billion in 1987 to ECU 12 billion in 1995.

The completion of the Single Market by 1993 calls for the liberalization of telecommunications inside the European Community and thereby the gradual abolition of national post and telegraph monopolies for most interconnected equipment as well as for all services except voice telephony and telex. This will stimulate technological progress, broaden the diversity of telecom services and raise their quality. It will lead to more intense competition and lower charges. Annual growth in the telecom market over the next four to six years is likely to develop along the following lines: 5 % annual increase in voice traffic and 22 % for data traffic.

By 1991 at the latest, data traffic already accounted for over half of world communications. About three quarters of all business communications would be via in-house communications infrastructure and the other quarter handled by public or privately owned wide-area networks. These momentous developments in the telecommunications field in Western Europe combined with ever advancing progress in computer and telecom technology are creating expanding markets for equipment and a variety of related services. This ensures a steady demand for consultancy, equipment and network development and training. To respond to these developments, "equipment producing/service providing" companies that combine diversified capacities in telecommunication and data processing have been springing up to provide tailormade integrated installations and services to their customers.

Thus, next to the major telecom equipment companies in Western Europe such as Siemens, Alcatel, Ericsson, ATT and General Electric (GB) there are more specialized groups which cater to the new demand by providing networking applications and information technology in the form of state of the art equipment combined with a broad range of related services, MHS *(message handling systems)*-applications and value added services.

Electronic information services are to be found in a large variety of applications. There are the widely known services offered by text and bibliographic online systems such as Dialog, Questel (scientific information) and Maxwell Infoline; those supplied by data and transactional online systems such as Reuters and Telekurs (financial information); and the important segment consisting of service industry on-line systems such as S.W.I.F.T. (interbank), SITA (inter airlines), ISTEL (travel agents), RESINTER (hotel booking), Visa and American Express (charge cards), CEDEL and Euroclear. Large companies such as news publishers (Maxwell, Bertelsmann, Reed, Elsevier), oil and chemical corporations (Shell, BP), car-hire companies and IBM have their own in-house online systems. Finally there are the public access services such as the videotext systems in many West European countries of which the most famous ones are Minitel in France, Prestel in the U.K., Bildschirmtext in Germany and the expanding array of bank ATMs. Once the dominant force in electronic information services, the public sector is gradually being overtaken by privately-owned services.

S.W.I.F.T., one of the new telecommunications ventures which started operations at the height of the first petroleum crisis, has established a world leadership in perfect quality telecommunications. Each day, S.W.I.F.T. transfers some 2 million messages among nearly 4,000 participating banks. Since the beginning of its operations, S.W.I.F.T. has never lost one message, a remarkable record which is statistically "impossible". By 1990, S.W.I.F.T. had reached a turnover of ECU 250 million. Mr. Bessel Kok, the driving force behind S.W.I.F.T.'s strategic change, has succeeded in creating a corporate culture which is without comparison. Joining S.W.I.F.T. is like joining a family. If you visit S.W.I.F.T. headquarters in the woods of La Hulpe some 15 minutes from the centre of Brussels, you will readily understand why.

The CIT Research report indicated that the much-vaunted market for value-added services generated turnover of a "mere" ECU 700 million in 1987, 71% of which was in the United Kingdom. However, this market segment is expected to grow to ECU 5 billion by 1995, with the relative U.K. share gradually decreasing to 37%.

Value Added Networks - VANs - are a permutation of data, voice and image communications which lead to a series of services ranging from a voice mailbox to a complete disaster recovery programme. The growth rate of VANs is currently 50% per year. By 1990, VAN services had generated an estimated ECU 2 billion of business in the United Kingdom alone. Today, there are already several hundred VANs operational in Great Britain.

Entrepreneurship in this market has but one limit: creativity. Direct Business Satellite Systems (DBSS), a new U.K. company, proposes to collect messages in electronic form from customers via telecommunications lines. It would then broadcast the data via satellite to small dish antennae in a matter of seconds and for as little as one penny per message. DBSS uses spare radio channels carried by Britain's first direct broadcasting television satellite launched in 1989. The service is targeted to organizations as diverse as bookmakers, insurance brokers, banks and security houses.

Data networking is used to move large volumes of computerized information - sales records, lists of clients, invoices, credit-card authorizations - between separate offices. The market for such data movement, worth ECU 3.5 billion in 1990, is expected to grow to ECU 10.5 billion by 1995 according to forecasts by CIT Research.

Companies that have set up their own network, mostly through leasing lines from telephone companies and connecting their computers, sell off their facilities to other companies in order to help cover the costs. Two of the largest data-networking services open to outside customers started this way. They are "GEIS", owned by General Electric, and IBM's "Information Network". British Telecom's network "Tymnet" was originally purchased from McDonnell Douglas in 1989. If, as may happen, it were strengthened by "Information Network", Tymnet would become one of the strongest operators in the market.

The German Bundespost has embarked on an ambitious programme to offer remote control systems for households using the telephone network infrastructure. Under this system, customers can check all appliances remotely by means of a telephone call. The hardware for the system was developed by Racal of the United Kingdom and the software by Dr. Neuhaus Group of West Germany. Ultimately, 6,000 municipalities will be hooked into the system network. Who claimed the German telecom authorities were insensitive to change?

The advent of telecommunications-based services is transforming societies everywhere, not only in Western Europe and North America.

A recent study on Sri Lanka indicated that the availability of rural telephone lines had permitted the country's farmers to keep up-to-date on quoted prices for their produce on the Colombo Exchange. The prices at which they could sell rose to 80% of the prevailing exchange prices instead of the 40 to 60% they had obtained previously.

The opportunities generated by the information society are certainly not limited to the developed world. The competitive edge in a service is man-made and, as such, it can be used as a tool for Third World development and regional development, the only precondition being that both entrepreneurs and policy-makers identify the opportunities and have faith in their ability to succeed.

17. Telemarketing Services

Direct marketing aims at creating and exploiting a direct relationship between the supplier and his customer or prospective customer without interposing any other intermediaries. Telemarketing is not only used for sales activities: telemarketing is a vital tool in the compilation and updating of databanks, the identification of personal sales call leads, and the facilitation of after-sales services.

Telemarketing opens up myriad possibilities. Thus, a company wishing to embark on a hostile takeover might call in a telemarketing team to contact shareholders over the weekend and persuade them to vote one way or the other at an extraordinary general meeting on the following Monday.

Telemarketing is a rapidly growing element within direct marketing services. The obvious distinguishing feature of telemarketing is that the communication medium involved is the telephone. The calls can be outbound, where the seller initiates the call, or inbound, where the consumer initiates the call. We are not talking about a very sophisticated business; it is at first sight not comparable with the telecom networks discussed above. The business responds to a clear need in the market and generates flexible employment for persons with limited qualifications but with great communication capacities.

The total telemarketing services turnover worldwide is estimated to be between ECU 3 and 6 billion. The European share is likely to top ECU 1.2 billion in 1992. The expected progress per year is 60%. Investments in telemarketing equipment and systems, basically flexible telephone systems and hands-free phones, toll-free numbers, fast and interactive computers, local area networks, dedicated lines and databases, is growing by 50 to 55% per annum. There are already an estimated 1,500 professional telemarketing offices in Europe. The prospects for growth are large as this figure is only 5% of the number of U.S. telemarketing service companies.

The impressive growth of telemarketing services is made possible by the widespread availability of telecommunications. Each company and approximately 90% of private homes have a phone. In the United Kingdom alone, some one million people have as a main job the making and receiving of calls. Therefore it is no surprise that up to 90% of advertisers claim that they use, or soon will use telemarketing services as part of their business communications strategy. 68% of companies operating with telemarketing services use these for customer services, 45% for lead generation.

Consumers and potential buyers are flooded with communications through advertising. It is becoming more and more difficult to get the attention of the prospect. Telemarketing permits extremely fine targeting to well determined market niches. The cost for one call is between ECU 4 and 5 for products and services which require no specialization, although the price can be as high as

ECU 20 for expert calls, for example in the area of pharmaceuticals, where the telephone marketeer must master pharmacological product terminology.

Wang sells its computer peripheral equipment and standard software to some 10,000 clients per telephone. Wang pays the agency DTM ECU 7 per direct contact call, i.e., a call which results in a conversation with the decision maker. Siemens has installed a 50-person strong telemarketing team in-house; Jacob Suchard promotes its new coffee through an agency and Melitta filters skims regularly per phone through 7,000 small pubs and restaurants searching for their needs as their turnover is too small to justify a personal call on a regular basis. Chase Manhattan Bank in Germany has no network of offices and resorts to telephone marketing to identify clients' needs.

Telemarketing services are not regulated at all in Europe except in Germany where it has been forbidden since 1970 to establish a first contact with a potential private person by phone. Calls to the office with the objective of selling products and services for private consumption are also forbidden. The result is that several German companies operate their telemarketing activities from Luxembourg, or Austria, where no such restrictions exist.

Telemarketing agencies diversify quickly into training. Decisions Group (United Kingdom), founded by Karen Darby at the age of 24, already generates more than 25% of its turnover in this area. After having performed a series of telemarketing assignments succesfully, clients may wish to upgrade the performance of their own telephone operators. The leading telemarketing companies have therefore established affiliated companies specialized in teaching telemarketing skills. This strategy creates client loyalty and broadens the overall market for telemarketing services. The telemarketeer will be called upon for large assignments which the basic team of a blue chip company cannot handle independently. Training is the key to successful telemarketing. 75% of all telemarketing personnel are given periodic training; no one arrives with a diploma in telemarketing. Personnel turnover remains large as only 25% of staff stay on for more than three years. Telemarketing is considered by 60% of employees as a stepping stone to career development and nearly all see their activity as a full-time job.

18. Quality and Inspection Control Services

The day to day smooth functioning of modern economies calls for multiple and systematic quality controls, measurements and analyses of goods, substances, equipment and processes. Such tasks are performed either by private firms, e.g. to check conformity with contract specification and private standards, or by public or semi-public organizations that check conformity with mandatory technical regulations under various statutes. The latter kind of control is also carried out by private firms that are accredited by public authorities to do so.

The size of this huge market is difficult to assess because of its highly diversified nature, the imprecision of the data, notably on the location of the provision of the service and, more generally, the absence of recorded statistics. At a rough guess, the turnover for such services in the European Community probably amounts to more than ECU 11 billion with employment over 200,000 persons.

British service industry experts have estimated that, in the United Kingdom some ECU 400 are spent every year per person on quality controls, testing, inspection and measurement activities. This figure however does not seem to represent the market for this service, but the overall direct and indirect cost to the consumer of ensuring quality, safety, respect of technical regulations, medical analysis, etc. Extrapolated over the whole of the EC, and taking into account the fact that not all Member States have attained the industrial and scientific development level of the United Kingdom, the overall cost for the Community might amount to some ECU 70 to 80 billion.

Quality control services take many forms. One of the major ones is commercial pre- and post-shipment inspection which is performed mainly in the course of international trade. Then there is testing by laboratories, statutory inspection (including passenger car and truck controls), classification of ships by control and certification organisations, calibration and miscellaneous activities such as second hand aircraft assessment, loss adjustment in insurance claims, etc.

The demand for such quality control services has been expanding rapidly on account of the spread of new technologies and materials and the multiplication of highly sophisticated products and production and building processes. Purchasing agents of all kinds are looking for quality assurance from these suppliers. As a result, there is expanding demand by companies for the certification of their quality assurance systems. Customers and indeed the salesmen themselves are no longer in a position to check quality, health and safety and are thus forced to rely on assurances of conformity via standards. They also expect rising standards in product quality. The rise of environmental preoccupations that call for controls on air, water and soil pollution and of toxic waste has contributed to the booming demand for this service which will remain a growth sector for years to come.

The largest companies offer a vast range of controls and checks as well as related technical and advisory services. Their business also includes overseeing of building and production processes and even extends to the checking of qualifications and skills of people occupied in specific sectors. Smaller private firms specialize in segments of the market such as laboratory analysis of specific substances or the checking of particular products or equipment with respect to sets of standards and technical regulations. Next to these private operators there are public or semi-public institutions with various statutory and often monopolistic assignments in the field of quality control and inspection.

With the unrelenting growth of legislative and regulatory initiatives for safety, health, quality and environmental purposes, there has been a corresponding rise in demand for controlling, monitoring and auditing all technical regulations that are being drawn up. A joint public sector/private sector approach has developed with a clear line of demarcation between the respective responsibilities.

The public sector draws up legislation and defines norms for a variety of products such as drugs, cosmetics, food additives, equipment and prototype approval systems such as for cars and car exhausts. The private sector or semi-public organizations are entrusted with testing, auditing, monitoring, data management and reporting. The two sectors collaborate to achieve their common goals; these include safety of workers, consumers and the public in general and the preservation of the environment.

The completion of the Community's internal market by 1993 will have an impact on the quality control service sector. Trade flows and economic growth should accelerate as should inspection work. In parallel, however, harmonization of standards and technical regulations as well as mutual recognition of testing is being pushed through and will thus help to reduce wasteful retesting. But the speed of progress in this area is hard to predict and it is therefore difficult to foresee whether the progressive elimination of much of this intra-EC retesting will be compensated by the overall growth in the demand for quality control due to market expansion, as well as to the increasing sophistication of products and production processes, to rising worries about environment and to the growing tendency of consumers to prefer products with a quality label. All in all, market growth and continued fierce competition in this service sector of the EC can be confidently predicted.

Certification consists in checking products and services in order to ascertain whether they conform with specifications, usually technical standards or regulations. The demand for certification comes from public authorities which wish to ensure that products or services on the market conform to regulations and from insurers and customers in general who wish to obtain quality and performance assurances.

Certification of products and services takes many forms. It may consist of a unilateral declaration by a manufacturer or provider of services that his product is in conformity with a given standard or set of standards. Normally, however, certification involves an outside party which may be a testing laboratory issuing official reports, or any qualified body or institution delivering marks of conformity or certificates of safety. The Kitemark of the British Standards Institute, DIN in Germany, AENOR and AFNOR respectively in Spain and France are some of the best known examples. In the latter case the issuer is generally an organisation approved or accredited by the public authorities to take responsibility for the safety of equipment and products. Such compulsory certification called statutory inspection applies typically to pressure vessels, boilers, tanks, lifts, cranes, bridges, gas and electrical installations, etc.,all of which represent possible hazards to workers or the general public.

In the Community there are more than 1,000 certification organizations which examine the quality of products and certify conformity with technical regulations on behalf of the public authorities.

The "Confédération Européenne d'Organismes de Contrôle" (CEOC), brings together a number of statutory inspection organizations from all West European countries except Greece, Ireland and Iceland. Most participants operate on a non-profit basis. They are recognized by the public regulatory bodies and provide engineering and other safety control services for a large variety of equipment such as boilers, lifts, electrical and heating installations and industrial plants. They also contribute to the drafting of standards and norms in association with ISO and CEN/CENELEC and enter into bilateral reciprocal agreements with inspection organisations in other countries, thus allowing for mutual recognition of such services.

Table 7-7.   **Major statutory inspection agencies in Europe**

AIB (Association des Industriels de Belgique) and Vinçotte	B
Arbejdstilsynet	DK
Asistencia Tecnica Industrial	E
Associated Offices Technical Committee	UK
Directoraat Generaal van de Arbeid	NL
Groupement des Apave	F
Istituto Superiore per la Prevenzione e la Sicurezza del Lavoro	I
Luxcontrol	L
TÜV (Technische Überwachungs-Vereine)	FRG

Source: author

One subsector in the area of controls and certification is calibration. As the objective assessment of quality and compliance with standards and technical regulation requires measurements in order to ensure the requisite accuracy, the measurement instruments themselves must be calibrated either directly or indirectly against internationally accepted primary measurements, standards of length, voltage, temperature, etc. Certificates of calibration are issued not only by national metrology laboratories but also by test laboratories and manufacturing companies which have been accredited as calibration laboratories.

The economic importance of calibration as a segment of quality control in terms of turnover and employment is difficult to assess. Estimates for the Italian market indicate that some 40 accredited organisations which engage in calibration activities issue some 2,500 certificates a year at the cost of some ECU 1,750 each. It is estimated that in some further 10,000 calibration certificates are issued every year in Italy on a private basis. Total turnover would therefore represent some ECU 20 million a year in Italy. In the United Kingdom some 200 laboratories thus issue close to 80,000 certificates annually. For the whole of the EC, the market may amount to over ECU 100 million.

Another subsector of quality control is in the field of maritime transportation where it is generally known as "classification" of ships and offshore structures. Specialized control and inspection companies provide a variety of services, ranging from classification (i.e., defining the characteristics and condition of ships), and checking of offshore structures to various kinds of statutory inspections for countries which have national regulations or subscribe to international conventions. As in commercial inspection, there are in this field of maritime transportation a number of very large European firms; Lloyds Register of Shipping from the United Kingdom, the Germanischer Lloyd of Germany and Det Norske Veritas of Norway are the market leaders. The companies engage in regulatory controls and inspection activities both in the Community and on behalf of foreign nations at the worldwide level.

In the Community, six companies, all European, conduct pre-shipment inspections. They are SGS, based in Switzerland, which is the leader in this field, Bureau Veritas and Socotec of France, Inchcape PLC from the United Kingdom (which operates through its affiliates, Intertek in the United States and Caleb Brett in the United Kingdom), Inspectorate of Switzerland through its "Audit Unit", and the much smaller Cotecna Inspection (also of Switzerland).

Shipment inspection services also sometimes extend to a number of other activities such as the drafting of contract documents, the interpretation of international sales contracts, advice on import and export regulations or arbitration services which consist in the inspection of goods, materials, equipment, installations and buildings.

The Société Générale de Surveillance, SGS-Group, based in Geneva is the world's largest inspection company. It is estimated that it inspects about 4% of world trade. SGS operates in 140 countries, including the twelve EC Member States, and owns 232 companies and 233 laboratories. Some 25,000 technicians, specialists and highly trained staff inspect, control and analyse all kinds of products and equipment. SGS has expanded its services to health care, environmental auditing, waste management and quality management consultancy. In 1990, its turnover reached about ECU 1.3 billion, about half of it in Western Europe.

In Germany the TÜV Technical Inspection Agencies (Technische Überwachungs-Vereine), are the major operators in the market for quality control and inspection. They are established as private organizations with the status of "registered associations" and perform tests, inspection and advisory services mainly in the fields of environmental protection and motor vehicle traffic. There are 11 TÜVs in Germany with 450 establishments for traffic safety alone (inspection of cars and light trucks) as well as one "Association of TÜVs" (Vereinigung der TÜV) which gathers the experience of all the TÜVs and makes it available to interested parties. The TÜVs have also set up regional establishments in all the Member States of the Community except Ireland and Denmark and in 17 other countries such as Canada, Japan, the USA, Turkey and South Africa. The TÜVs also engage in initial and continuous in-service training. They employ at present 13,500 people, about 9,200 of them with a university degree or technical diploma. Also members of the TÜV association are five companies with their own inspection facilities, including the three large chemical firms Bayer, Hoechst and BASF.

Technical control assistance is given by specialized companies or organizations for the design and construction of electricity generating plants and equipment (e.g., KEMA in the Netherlands, Lloyd's Register in the United Kingdom), the building of railways and of telecom networks, the construction of refineries, rational use of energy, etc. Second hand industrial installations and transportation equipment such as aircraft can be checked to guarantee quality and assess the risks of breakdown or failure. Safety audit services are offered to check safety policy effectiveness of companies for fire and explosion prevention.

Loss adjusting in insurance consists of damage survey services for the insurance sector. This is performed either on behalf of the insurer or for the insured party and entails the investigation of claims, evaluation of loss, interpretation of insurance policies and recommendations concerning settlement. A wide range of assets, from real estate to motor vehicles, is covered. In France for example, Galtier Expertises and Roux have a leading position in the market on behalf of the insured parties. In the United Kingdom, Robins Davies and Little of the SGS Group are the leaders in the supply of this service on behalf of insurance companies.

With product quality becoming an ever more critical element in competitiveness and corporate image creation, many firms have gone into total quality control which aims at defect prevention going as far as zero defects. All this leads to systematic laboratory testing and quality auditing throughout the production process. This type of consultancy service has been growing explosively, with demand coming from across the spectrum of industry and services. Several of the larger companies in the quality control sector have entered this new market and issue "certificates of management systems" that confirm the reliability of the quality assurance system set up by companies and conformity of the quality system to the appropriate standards. ISO 9000 has been trendsetter and will most likely spur many service corporations to invest heavily.

This chapter has provided only a glimpse of the myriad service sectors which have demonstrated a capacity to grow consistently at double-digit rates. The list is by no means comprehensive: in fact, the companies, the entrepreneurs and the sectors quoted here represent little more than the tip of the iceberg.

By way of conclusion, let us ask a simple question: who among us would ever have imagined that funeral services could be internationalized?

The French funeral services group Pompes Funèbres Générales (PFG) has acquired a 29% stake in Kenyon Securities, the third-largest quoted funeral services group in the United Kingdom. The French group now has interests in Belgium, Switzerland, North Africa and Singapore. The U.K. market for this service is 25%-controlled by the Co-operative Wholesale Society, together with three quoted companies - Hodgson Holding, Great Southern Group and Kenyon Securities.

It appears that internationalization was PFG's only route to expansion now that the mortality rate in France is declining. The French group's expansion into other markets imparts new meaning to the phrase "funeral services"...

CHAPTER EIGHT

A New Approach to Management

The new approach to management is based on how some twenty European services companies have succeeded in expanding at unprecedented rates.

Managing growth is exciting. Twinning industry and services is very promising. Few have experience, even fewer have succeeded.

Managing in a services context requires a whole new approach. But if today's corporate leaders in services take their cue from gurus who have made their reputation on the back of the manufacturing sector, then they run the risk of mortgaging the entire future of their businesses, both in services and manufacturing.

Ever since the first oil shock back in 1973 there has been heated discussion about one key management issue: how to secure a competitive edge in a progressively global marketplace? That is exactly what this final chapter is all about.

Management gurus have emerged from every nook and cranny of manufacturing industry, postulating macro-theories and handing out prescriptions for specific sectors of industry - textiles, automotive, electronics, chemicals, pharmaceuticals, and so on.

The typical CEO's bookcase is crammed with management literature. And every mail delivery brings a shower of invitations to management courses, conferences, workshops, seminars, briefings, and the like.

And what do all these publications and all these courses and conferences have in common?

Quite simply this: with precious few exceptions, they all focus on manufacturing industry. The only real exceptions to the rule are specialist conferences on the financial services industry. After all, it was only in March 1991 that the renewed Management Center Europe held a three-day conference for top executives on "Successful Service Management". Many industrialists participated, but only one speaker came from the leading service corporations in Europe: Claus Møller, the founder-chairman of TMI from Denmark, a management guru himself.

Recipes for the successful management of a services sector are decidedly thin on the ground. This is all the more astonishing given that the services sector represents a clear majority of today's enterprises. And, as we have seen, services are the only area of the economy with broad perspectives for massive growth and of key importance to industry as well.

That said, there is some justification - or, at worst, explanation - for this decidedly dismissive treatment of the services sector. The plain fact is that most services are structured so as to be provided and used at the same time and in the same place. This is what really distinguishes services from manufactured goods: it is highly unusual for manufactured goods to be produced and used on-the-spot and simultaneously. Without wishing to be too philosophical about it, the fundamental distinction between services and manufactures belongs in the realm of the space/time continuum.

None of the above suggests that there are **no** lessons that the services sector can profitably learn from manufacturing. They are good, but simply not good enough. And frankly speaking, if only all service companies could be managed like the best in manufacturing industry it would be a massive improvement. But this chapter is not about improving: it is about growth, competitive edges, outstanding performance and how to achieve it!

Value-Added: The Name of the Game

The ultimate objective of any enterprise is to create value-added in the hands of the consumer or end-user.

It follows that the only way to develop and retain a competitive edge is to deliver products and services which have an optimal value-added content.

This is by no means a startlingly original observation. The value-added debate has raged for several years, not least one suspects because the Japanese have become increasingly key players on world markets. And it has become apparent that they seem to have developed a concept of value-added which we in the Western Hemisphere find progressively difficult to match.

Conventional management theory identifies three methods by which value-added can be enhanced: increased productivity, quality improvement, and the application of "just-in-time".

The efficient use of professional services emerges as a fourth indispensable element in developing a genuine competitive edge. What is more, using professional services will increasingly become the important factor.

If the efficient use of professional services is recognized as a cornerstone of modern management philosophy throughout this decade and into the next millennium, there will be a typical "chicken-and-egg" situation. In fact, services will become more professional and more sophisticated as the need for progressively professional and sophisticated services becomes apparent.

Clearly, productivity, quality and timeliness are three key factors which permeate any business with aspirations to reach the top and stay there. But, in a market characterized by over-supply in goods and where the client has the choice, professional services will make the difference.

Let's look at this in some more detail.

Productivity

When Japanese manufacturers made their first inroads into Western markets back in the 1970s, it suddenly dawned on management experts in both Europe and North America that we in the West have a serious productivity problem.

It did not escape our attention that the Japanese automotive industry was capable of turning out twice or even three times more cars than we could - using as many or even fewer employees and production-line workers.

It was no coincidence that General Motors committed over ECU 45 billion in the course of a decade to step up productivity at its plants. That would probably have been enough back in 1975 to buy Toyota outright.

The quest for productivity inevitably led to crash programmes involving computerization and telecommunications technologies. Thousands of delegations trekked eastwards towards the Land of the Rising Sun to gaze in rapture and astonishment upon Japan's automated production lines. They conveniently forgot (if they ever knew) that the world's first robots were developed in Europe and in the United States. Unfortunately, we were better at developing the concept than applying it to our own production processes.

Now, twenty years on, we are all "into" automation.

There is hardly a small-to-medium size enterprise anywhere in Europe that does not have at least a couple of computers or a few electronically-controlled pieces of plant.

What we must ask, of course, is whether it was all too little and too late.

Quality

For all our efforts to boost productivity, our industries here in Europe and over in North America still seemed unable to match the competitive edge secured by the Japanese.

Then, at the beginning of the 1980s, a new buzzword started to make the rounds: quality.

The Japanese had it, and we were told we had to get it. Accordingly, management was awash with quality theory - quality management, total quality control, quality circles, and what have you. How many times were we encouraged to see quality as a panacea?

Organizations mushroomed: the European Organization for Quality, the European Foundation for Quality Management, the Flemish/Spanish/British Centre for Quality, and so on - all of them dedicated to one thing, namely turning our ailing industries round on the basis of quality principles.

It seemed rather obvious at the time. Irrespective of how productive a particular manufacturer happened to be, he would lose that vital competitive edge if another manufacturer in his sector could offer a better-quality product range - even if the price was higher.

The client has a choice. Our consumers are faced with an embarrassment of riches, unlike our contemporaries in the centrally-planned economies of Central and Eastern Europe, where the Western system of supply and demand is unheard of. There, you buy what is available.

Suddenly, we were producing more efficiently *and* emphasizing quality. Surely this would be enough to attract foreign investment? Particularly now that we had manufacturing workforces which were quality-trained, quality-conscious and quality-oriented?

Today, General Motors turns out automobiles with defect ratios every bit as low as its Japanese rivals. But, lo and behold, it still isn't enough to knock the Japanese off their perch.

What we needed was to take another leaf out of the Japanese book: just-in-time management.

Just-in-Time

The next wave of investment would not be in productivity and quality alone, it would feature just-in-time management principles. Production without inventory, with raw materials, semi-finished products and finished products delivered by or warehoused by third parties. Meanwhile, manufacturers would focus on what they do best: manufacturing.

Kanban now became the slogan. A fresh school of management gurus latched on to this latest Japanese buzzword as the philosopher's stone.

There is a lot to be said for inventory minimization. What cannot be said about it, however, is that it is the key to corporate success. It is a key to survival.

Transnationally active enterprises noticed very quickly that they had not only to site their facilities at low-cost locations, they also had to find low-cost but effective distribution centres. Clearly, not every product or spare part was kept at every location: it made sense to opt for a central location and use an express delivery service such as DHL to expedite the product or part to the customer. Sadly, however, courier services may be able to cope with spare parts and documents, but the situation becomes more difficult when it comes to semi-finished and finished goods.

The simple truth is that we in the West cannot compete with the Japanese when it comes to just-in-time delivery.

This is not because we are congenitally incapable of adapting our industries in this way. Not at all: Japanese manufacturers operating in Europe and North America have also decided against pushing the *kanban* approach to the lengths which obtain in Japan. Our transport, warehousing and distribution infrastructure is, to put it bluntly, not capable of 100% application of the just-in-time principle. Additionally, distributors in Europe and North America are not typically located immediately next to the manufacturers they serve, as is the case in Japan. In short, after a thousand or so delegations had visited Japan, there developed a consensus that just-in-time *à la japonaise* was simply not practicable in our marketplace, however laudable the concept might be in principle. The Japanese, it seems, recognized this some time ago.

Nevertheless, the fact remains that corporate survival and corporate success are served by producing to the highest quality standard attainable, distributing as efficiently as the marketplace permits, and delivering as quickly as possible.

The time factor has also been invoked in relation to the capacity to crunch out new products and models. Responsiveness to the market is an engine of competitiveness. During the past 14 months, Toyota has added six new models to its line of 59 vehicles. Over one half of the products manufacturerd by Siemens and a quarter of 3M's product catalogue are less than five years old. Hewlett-Packard perhaps tops this with more than 50% of turnover in 1991 coming from products which were introduced three years ago or less. Often the key question asked in industry is how fast someone can respond to changing trends on the market.

Technology has often been referred to as a deus ex machina. But, technology is today available to all. We could ask ourselves, if even the Taiwanese and the Koreans are capable of producing chips more successfully than the Europeans, what is the importance of technologies? All types of technologies are quickly available to all key players on the market. A leading IBM executive concludes that the billions in R&D which Big Blue invests are enough to maintain the competitive position of Big Blue. It is certainly not going to create a key advantage anymore. Those were the 70s and the 80s, now we are shaping up for the 21st century. It came as no surprise that IBM eagerly chip agreements with Apple and Siemens in summer 1991.

The timing of technological breakthroughs is also crucial. If you invent a new chip, you have spent half a billion ECU. Then, you have to spend another half a billion to be able to produce it. If your manufacturing scheme is six months behind schedule, then you have a pretty expensive warehouse for an obsolete technology. It all moves so fast, and technology is so important, but no miracles can be expected. The advantage is that one may lose out today in one technology, but enjoy a six-month advance in another system, enabling you to leapfrog once more your competitors.

Services: The Cornerstone of the 1990s and Beyond

The comparison of services and industry is summarized in Table 8.2 on pages 147-148. Behind each characteristic mentioned you will find a number which refers to the comparison in the table. There are a total of 50 comparisons summarized.

It should not be forgotten that up to 75% of the value added in the manufacture of an automobile is generated by services to production. In the case of agriculture, this ratio can even be as high as 95%. In the steel industry, services to production are determinant for 50% of the eventual sales price.

It follows that manufacturing industry and agriculture must be able to count on fast and flexible access to professional services.

Without labouring the point, it is as well to recall that management has been agonizing over productivity, quality and just-in-time when these three features are impacting on *less than half* of product value-added. We can perhaps be forgiven for arguing, therefore, that it is high time that management took a long, hard look at the other side of the business, if only to acknowledge the key role that professional services can play in day-to-day and strategic management of an enterprise.

When we talk of "services", we are not simply referring to the upper end of the market providing sophisticated services such as software development, design or engineering inputs, we are also looking at more mundane aspects such as cleaning and maintenance, security, human resources, and so on.

A recent study by the European Service Industries Forum (ESIF) has demonstrated that no less than 20% of manufacturing industry's service needs can be contracted out-of-house. By doing just that, manufacturing industry secures access to services which are specialized and efficient without incurring the costs implicit in developing them in-house.

Modern managers would do well to bear in mind all four cornerstones of value-added: management that fails to do so will only be holding the door open to its competitors.

Competitive strength in the 1990s and beyond will depend, therefore, on the integration of four elements into our corporate strategies: productivity, quality, efficient and timely distribution, and *services*.

This book has clarified at length and in some detail that these services are growing at double - digit growth (1). Most of the sectors enjoy low barriers of entry (3) and governments in general do not intervene in their operations (5). The problem of course remains that there is hardly any market data available (6) which fuels demand for market research. These professional services thus are different from manufacturing industry, which is characterized by low growth and high barriers to entry while the government intervenes at every possible (and impossible) moment. The fact that industry is so well documented, especially by the national institutes for statistics, may in this sense be considered a disadvantage. Everyone is in the picture: there are no "secrets" anymore.

Business Support Services

The potential for business support services is enormous.
Today, U.S. manufacturing industry buys in 8% of its services; in the United Kingdom, by contrast, only 4% of services are bought in at present. In Japan - need one say it? - manufacturers typically belong to a *keiretsu*, an informal holding company, from within whose ranks they can draw up to 15% or so of the professional services they require.
It is not surprising that business support services are the fastest-growing sector of the European economy. The vast majority of these services are currently growing at 10%-plus annually, hence the appellation "double-digit growth companies".
The management approach described in the following is based on some five years' research conducted by the author as chief executive of ESIF, a network of successful European service companies. On the basis of in-depth study of more than 50 services sectors, ESIF has identified what the management of successful services is all about and how it differs so radically from conventional management.

A World of Difference

Even the most cursory analysis immediately reveals one salient fact: that services across a broad spectrum are significantly more "productive" than commonly expected.
Conventional wisdom holds that "productivity" is irrelevant in any discussion of the tertiary sector.
This is totally unacceptable. Worse, it illustrates a total disregard for and ignorance of the dynamics of the services function.
In fact, services of every description - ranging from cleaning and maintenance to the most sophisticated information technology - have exhibited a staggering growth in "productivity" over the course of the past decade. Furthermore, the trend will continue.
What is difficult, of course, is to find a basis for comparison of productivity in the conventional sense as used by manufacturing industry and "productivity" as present in and generated via the services sector.
As we have seen, services that were initially in-house and have subsequently

been externalized are not directly comparable.

The world leader in cleaning and maintenance - ISS of Denmark - can clean 300 to 400 m2 per hour in accordance with strict parameters. Comparing ISS with an in-house team of cleaners is clearly inadmissible. Nor is it admissible to argue that ISS "costs more": it all depends on how "costs" are calculated. Is it productive to have a team of in-house cleaners with no specialized skills? Is it productive to retain cleaning personnel in-house, bearing in mind the attendant social security costs, the annual bonus, and the training they must receive?

In practice, it is difficult to make a case to the effect that ISS is anything other than *less* expensive.

What is more, real productivity goes *up* when outside professionals are called in, if only for the statistical reason that the workers retained are allocated to productive tasks rather than unproductive ones.

A similar pattern emerges at the other end of the market. S.W.I.F.T., the Belgian based company that provides state-of-the-art international financial transfer services on behalf of banks and financial institutions, can hardly be claimed to cost more than what those banks and institutions used to pay when they effected such transactions in-house.

A S.W.I.F.T. message today is billed at BF 16 - several times lower then the cost of a telexed message ten years ago. At the same time, S.W.I.F.T. offers its client base a standardized, professional communications system, together with ancillary benefits such as more flexibility and enhanced message security.

Even ignoring the lower price-per-message charged by S.W.I.F.T. and the cost of maintaining separate and individual in-house personnel to perform the same function, can one genuinely argue that S.W.I.F.T.'s contribution to the operation is "unproductive"?

Certainly not.

Organizational Technology

A word is in order with respect to organizational technology (31).

Services have not become more productive because of new inventions, new product or process technologies. That is something that belongs in the realm of manufacturing industry.

In effect, services have become more productive because their management has taken steps to perfect a particular service or set of services to the point where an organizational technology is created.

Let's be clear on this: copying a key does not require a doctorate in mechanical engineering. But there is only one firm in the world - Minit International - that copies each year sixty million different keys worldwide at 4,700 outlets.

Nor is it admissible to assume that organizational technology is exclusively linked to the availability of computers or communications technology. There is no high-tech implicit in copying keys or cleaning factory floors. How much information technology is needed to prepare a Big Mac?

Singapore Airlines, Thai and Cathay Pacific have no access whatsoever to the best aerospace technologies. The Americans and the Soviets which control the world's aerospace technologies have lost market share in all segments of commercial airlines. Not one of the Asian airlines benefits from interest rate subsidies. Still these airlines are the world's favorite. Who did not try to imitate their marketing or personnel strategy? Noone seems capable of beating their organizational technology based on superior service.

In the table below, we attempt to provide an overview of what is really meant by organizational technology.

Table 8-1. **Organizational technologies**

1. Management skills	11. Quality controls
2. Marketing techniques	12. Personnel motivation
3. Distribution networks	13. Design integration
4. Training methods	14. Hierarchical division
5. Research methodologies	15. After sales services
6. Advertising schemes	16. Political engineering
7. Purchasing procedures	17. Contact and introductions
8. Information systems	18. Community programmes
9. Office structures	19. Communication capabilities
10. Decision making	20. Life style services

Source: author

Each single element of an organizational technology can be copied. The perfectly intertwined, fine tuned and interdependent system of elements can as a whole not be copied. Even if it is hard to distinguish a Big Mac from a Big Whopper, it has not been possible to imitate the organizational technology developed and improved by McDonalds. Personnel management cannot be patented and, more importantly, there is no reason to patent it.

This does not mean that service companies are not interested in technologies or in the protection of their intellectual property. On the contrary, it must be stated clearly that services do not *develop* technologies. Instead, the strength of a services company lies in its ability to *use* available technologies (32). There is immensely more added value created by *using* high tech than by *inventing* it.

The competitive edge of a service company depends on its people, its organizational technology and its capacity to use existing computer and telecommunication technologies (2). Here is the need to develop and design the infrastructure service companies require in order to operate (33). Manufacturing industry can rely to a very large extent on public utilities (electricity, water, road networks, railroads, etc.), but the typical services group is obliged to rely on its own infrastructure. Information technologies and telecommunications components are absolutely indispensable.

In the initial stages, a start-up services company can get by on the basis of a modest personal computer network and by using the conventional services provided by the national telecommunications authority. But, sooner rather than later, the firm will have to make a move into customized, dedicated IT and communications systems.

Unfortunately, the leading information technology and telecommunications companies have been strangely slow to appreciate the specific requirements of fast-growing service companies. This is why services companies themselves have often been obliged to develop their own applied technologies (32).

To recall an earlier example: when Federal Express was on the lookout for a small computer with barcode reading, processing and communications features, no single major manufacturer was particularly keen to cooperate. After all, they may have reasoned, courier services were too small a market segment to become involved with. Left to its own devices - literally! - Federal Express did a little tinkering and came up with a piece of equipment known today as the "supertracker". This is a handy little computer which reads off barcodes, feeds the information automatically into a central computer and permits permanent monitoring of each stage of every shipment. DHL now uses the same system. Neither company invented the component technology, of course, they simply made it work to their specific requirements.

In manufacturing industry, protecting product or process technology is one method of keeping a step ahead of the competition. Access to the market can be blocked for years by registering intellectual property rights and protecting the inventor by a labyrinth of patents and copyrights.

In the services sector, this is rarely the case (7). Even McDonalds has not taken the trouble to patent either its marketing processes or its personnel policies. Minit International manufactures its own equipment - and sells it to the competition. Group 4 Securitas, the European market leader in security systems, manufactures much of its own equipment, but has no hesitation in offering it for sale to its competitors.

And why not?

Imitating one aspect of a product or a process does not give the competitor full insight into the totality of the concept. What is more, an "open-door" policy as practised in the services sector enables individual firms to take the temperature of the marketplace and refine their own organizational technology accordingly. To put it bluntly, taking the lead in collaborating with competitors can offer a competitive edge.

The computer industry has finally understood that strategy. After years of building in isolation, they have agreed on an open system which should permit users to buy any hardware and run open system software on it. The mobile communication system in Europe has also learned to cooperate, and the television industry has finally come to an understanding of sorts on HDTV (high definition television). Whereas this compromise is sweetened by ECU 500 million from the EC Commission, this strategy of cooperation and competition has been the rule of the game in successful services for decades.

Another time and technology strategy of the manufacturing industry is to prolong as much as possible the product life cycle. This is an important way to improve bottom-line results by making the best out of cash cows. As soon as the life cycle cannot be extended anymore, then the "dogs are dumped". In services, numerous successful companies actually plan obsolesence (23) of their services early on. The reason is simple: market demand changes so rapidly that, if you hang on to what was good in the past, then your competitors may very well benefit from your resistance to change. When S.W.I.F.T. announced its first system, it announced at the same time the S.W.I.F.T. II system, creating a sense of discontinuity which forced the company to follow a client strategy and not a product strategy (11). This is most likely the most difficult turnaround in industrial management that is needed to make manufacturing successful in competing on the basis of their excellence in services.

Service Quality

The relationship between purchaser and vendor or manufacturer and distributor is radically different in the services sector from what we have grown accustomed to in manufacturing industry.

Clear evidence of this comes in the context of "quality".

Service quality is judged by the customer and it is impossible to apply objective standards and measures to determine if you have fulfilled the client's quality expectations. In the first place, isolating clearly the quality expectations in services is a very difficult task. The highly successful Danish tour operator Spies was very blunt in telling its prospective clients that hotel rooms in Spain would be lousy, and that their flight down there would be rough, with an uncertain departure time and an even less sure time of arrival. But the package was available for a ridiculously low price. Spies met the expectations of the client and even made money in the process.

Still, it has become clear over the past few years that quality is most valued by clients. According to numerous surveys, the client is even willing to pay more if he *believes* that the service supplier will better meet his quality expectations (29). In industry, the quality of a product is clearly determined by a broad set of technical specifications. In such a marketing environment, price is most often the key decisive factor.

One way of overcoming the quality dilemma is to undertake an audit of the actual cost to the client to achieve the results (26) he wishes to obtain. Throughout this process, it will become clear to both parties what objectives the client actually proposes. Very likely, while doing this, he will be in a position to fine tune his requests and preferences and even make adjustments according to the price indications that emerge. This audit implies that you are present when the needs (14) arise, otherwise your competitors will have taken care of the problem. In other words, one must have have a client strategy (11) so that the challenges can be met as soon as the contract is signed (15). Purchasing is the process (25), not production.

Essentially, a service is produced and delivered on-the-spot and without delay, unlike in manufacturing industry, where goods are produced, stocked, distributed to wholesalers, passed down through the distribution chain to retailers, and so on.

The upshot is that manufacturers have time on their side to correct faults and eliminate shortcomings in their production process. By contrast, one chance is usually all you have in a services context: it is *always* too late to repair fences. Therefore, the entire management concept is different. When you buy a new car and something goes wrong with it, the garage will effect repairs on the basis of the manufacturer's warranty. In other words, an efficient after-sales service can ensure that a dissatisfied customer is not lost for good. Solving his or her problem quickly and efficiently can even have the opposite effect, by helping establish customer loyalty.

This is simply not possible in the services sector.

Imagine the situation where your accountant gives you an incorrect balance sheet and cash flow projection for the new investment you have to present to your Board of Directors. It could well be that the selfsame accountant has performed sterling service over the previous ten years, but this one zero too many is enough to end the relationship - for good.

Similarly, a travel agent books you and your family into a miserable hotel, and you were not looking for cheap holiday. It may be possible to claim your money back, but your vacation plans have been ruined.

What it boils down to is that the quality of service must be as near to what the client has imagined for himself. In manufacturing industry, quality is a goal; in services it is a precondition. That is why in manufacturing industry nerves set in when the contract is about to be signed; in services, nerves will start really playing up when the contract is signed and one has to live up to the expectations (15).

In the absence of quality, the impression left at customer level is invariably negative. Worse, if one aspect of a service fails to come up to scratch, then the service as a whole is perceived to be deficient: when the parts which are multiplied together include just one zero, then the whole equation is reduced to zero (28).

A classic example: you arrive at a hotel, the reception staff are impeccable, your reservation is in order, you even get upgraded at a discount price. You have an excellent dinner with a superb wine, you check out without having to wait the following morning. There is a taxi available on the rank outside and the doorman gives you a friendly wave as you set off for the airport, in ample time to catch your flight. There is only one thing that you remember, however: the shower head was broken and there was no warm water.

Or what about the following scenario? You drive up to the hotel, the porter parks your car and you tip him accordingly. Next morning, when you are checking out, you discover that the porter has forgotten to give you back your car keys. Worse, he is off duty today and tomorrow. You may shrug it off on the grounds that these things happen, but that is one hotel stay you won't forget in a hurry.

Studies show that the majority of dissatisfied customers for services don't complain, they simply don't come back for more. When there is a problem with a product, there is usually a solution - a refund, a free repair service or whatever - and manufacturers who track complaints registered about their products actually secure an edge - they have a chance to make adjustments accordingly. When you are running a service operation, however, the chances are that you will never get to hear of what is going wrong. The customer often leaves without bothering to report the cause of his dissatisfaction. Faults remain uncorrected because they are largely undetected. Each dissatisfied customer takes the trouble to inform 24 persons, whereas each fully satisfied clients informs only 6 potential buyers.

Clearly, therefore, service companies have very good reason to put quality at the top of their list of priorities. Another reason is that it has become increasingly difficult to insure yourself against the bad performance of your service. In industry, most warranties are covered by an insurance contract which has been calculated in the price (30). But who knows the risk of a faulty communication at S.W.I.F.T. given that no message has even been lost? What is the damage done when a pre-shipment inspection of a ship with 400,000 tons of crude oil has revealed the wrong grade? Service companies must rely on a system of self-control (27) because recourse to insurance is not only unpractical, it is also very expensive.

Self-Control

In a manufacturing environment, there are invariably quality inspectors whose job it is to monitor product and process parameters. This is part of the administrative infrastructure, and anywhere between 30% and 40% of executive time is spent checking other people's work.

This principle, valid as it is in a manufacturing context, is worthless in a service situation. Given the one-place, one-time nature of services, the person directly responsible for performing that service is the only one to monitor his or her own quality. By the time someone else comes along to monitor service quality, it is too late.

There is a particular advantage which accrues to service industries in this respect, of course, to the extent that management doesn't spend a huge chunk of its time checking up and following through. Instead, it does what it is supposed to do: it manages.

The self-monitoring function entails a whole list of related matters. What if a colleague spots a mistake or a shortcoming? What if a particular task or service does not fall within your area of competence? What if you are the only person on hand to remedy a particular situation which is not of your making? These questions can only be answered correctly when the company offers its personnel a loose and flat hierarchy (40) as well as accepting that employees *can* fail in any new initiative they are taking for the first time (39).

In effect, employees in the services sector must be prepared not only to discharge their own responsibilities but also to take it upon themselves to tackle on their own initiative situations which, strictly speaking, are outwith their area of responsibility. In services, the client always holds you reponsible, anytime, anywhere for anything (47).

In the best sense of the term, service employees are "multidisciplinary" (21). They have to be able to tackle different functions, even if it is not their immediate responsibility. But, in the wake of responding to the need of a client, why can't the cashier be a porter for a moment. How often have you been told by a sales representative that it is up to you to call the maintenance department to solve a problem with equipment he has sold you? Employees of the best service companies have to be able to react promptly and effectively to input and impressions from customers and colleagues alike.

It is something of a paradox that, in the context of services, the most common interface with the client more often than not occurs at the level of the least trained staff - the delivery boy, the switchboard operator, the receptionist. These persons are, so to speak, the antennae of the firm. To put it another way, personnel training and grooming cannot simply be restricted to the sales and marketing staff; instead, it must be directed towards the whole of the workforce.

In manufacturing industry, this is desirable. In the context of services, it is a *must*. You are staying at a hotel. Everything is running smoothly: this time around, there is hot water for the shower and the concierge has your car keys. Then, when you finally check out, you discover that there is no one around to help you with your luggage. The cashier, who has just presented you with your bill - and a hefty one at that - immediately takes in the situation. He has a choice: to send yet another in-house memorandum to the assistant general manager informing him that an additional porter is required, or to do something directly.

If he chooses the first option, the hotel will have lost yet another customer. Assuming that no-one else is waiting to check out, however, he also has the option of leaving his post for a second or two and helping you with your luggage. Clearly, he is going outside his sphere of responsibility. But you can bet your bottom dollar that the customer will appreciate the gesture. And that the customer will come back.

In services, an eye for detail is paramount (50). If your workforce does not develop this, the objective of 100% quality is a pipedream. Meeting the quality standards set forth by your client and developing a system of self control depends in the first place on appropriate human resources management, the cornerstone of success.

Human Resources Management

Human resources management is the key to management of services. This must be stressed time and time again. After all, human resources is all you have in a service company. And, each evening, your capital walks out of the front door and you hope that, next morning, it will come back. Human resources management is not so much about diplomas and experience, however as about attitudes and behaviour (43).

In much the same way as the marketing gurus of the 1960s used to argue that marketing was everybody's concern, from top management down, today's services stand or fall by the quality of personnel. Just as everyone had to be a marketeer, now everyone in service companies should be in charge of personnel (20).

In the final analysis, of course, it comes down to the simple notion that, if everyone does his or her job responsibly and effectively, taking care to match the customer's expectations, then a decentralized services group (24) can be confident of outpacing the competition. This decentralization can extend up to the level of non-existence of headquarters (35)

This is the case with BET, a diversified U.K. services enterprise with 140,000 employees. BET has no fewer than 5,000 outlets - and a headquarters operation which employs a mere 100 persons. ISS has just 45 staff in Copenhagen and the

European headquarters in London oversee 50,000 employees with just 6 persons. Yet a similar-size enterprise in the manufacturing sector would occupy a multi-storey office block.

This also sends an important message to the client: "You don't have to pay for flashy and expensive overheads, you pay for service and that is what you came for in the first place".

In a service context, staff are called upon to exhibit a wide range of expertise - not only in terms of professional qualifications and work experience, but also in terms of overall attitude and communication skills. This should not be mis-construed, however: there is no implication that no further schooling is neces-sary.

Quite the contrary: the need for on-the-job development is both essential and self-evident. At the same time, and bearing in mind that the majority of business support services are new, it is clear that one cannot count on years of experience. And, as the market evolves rapidly, the company should permit fast career progress as well. (42) If you have never imagined that you were so good in three dimensional video imaging then would it not be a pitty that you should first get through your three year introductory programme - like many banks impose - before you can get on with what you are discovering to be your strenghts?

When Genios, the leading German database company, acquired the services of an ex-*Financial Times* marketing manager, the latter had a track record that dated back only a modest five years. Obviously, there was no-one with 20 years' experience in database marketing. Similarly, diplomas in telemarketing are hard to come by.

Rapidly changing market conditions, the need to anticipate client requirements and a continuing obligation to evaluate competitor strengths and weaknesses - all of these presuppose adaptive, flexible and committed personnel. Which degree guarantees you such first-class colleagues? Which type of continuous education programme offers a quick fix for this challenge?

In a decentralized operation, it is unnecesary for a human resources manager to be familiar with every employee and all of his or her strengths and shortcomings. In practice, service companies - and, on occasion, even manufacturing compa-nies - encourage their staff to decide for themselves what they need to learn to be successful in their job (48). The company will then ensure that they are pointed in the right direction, towards an appropriate training course or towards another division in the company where they are eager to have someone willing to learn on the job with the client in a new market segment no one really fully understands. It is in this context that the service companies have to invest so heavily in time (17). We can apply the old advertising dilemma to training "I know that half of my budget is wasted, but I do not know which half!".

Communication Skills

Successful service companies all invest heavily in communication skills (44). There are no exceptions to this golden rule. This is only to be expected, given that services are a people-to-people affair, where good communication is central to efficiency and, as a result, cannot be left to chance.

In manufacturing industry, it has become largely inescapable that everyone speaks English in addition to his or her own mother tongue. In services, however, it is absolutely essential to speak the client's language (45). This means that we have to clearly understand the business of the client, his priorities and limitations so that this can be translated into a sound response from the company. How often do the subordinates only speak the language of their boss? The sales team will have to defend the interest of the client each time the company pursues a typical product strategy and speak up with his interests in mind.

A second universal language requirement in the services context is computer language (46). After all, this is the only language which everyone understands and which can streamline communications in an internationally oriented company with a global reach.

There is a third language - one that, in Europe, is all too often neglected: the language of the *smile*.

In a communication situation, laughter and smiles are easily applied when everything is going smoothly. When a problem arises, however, a quick smile is often invaluable in providing reassurance that everything is under control. Sadly, it is all too frequently the case that, when a problem crops up, the first reaction is to reach for the telephone and call someone higher up.

This is tantamount to passing the buck. Worse, it is passing the buck in the presence of the customer. While the latter may be impressed by this aggressive approach and straight talking, he is still stuck with the problem, waiting for someone to provide a solution.

The ability to communicate is, without doubt, one of the most vital aspects of the services business. The reasons are self-evident. Language skills, an ability to communicate effectively and easily in a face-to-face situation, familiarity with the techniques implicit in telephony, video, television and the like, the ability to be a good listener - all of these are skills intrinsic to services, a people-to-people business.

The "customer is king". But how can the customer be king if the workforce is treated like serfs? Somehow, the company has to put its own people first (9).

All-the-Time vs. Just-in-Time

The third key principle advocated by today's management gurus is the "just-in-time" principle.

Typically, just-in-time management implies that the entire distribution pattern within a company be exhaustively analyzed, taking account of raw materials flow, semi-finished product flow, finished product flow, and so on. Plants are closed down, distribution centres are shuffled around, the number of distributors is adjusted.

"Just-in-time" is the manufacturing industry's watchword. In services, however, "just-in-time" is not enough. Instead, the focus has to be on "all-the-time" (16). One of the principal reasons why companies contract out services is that senior management requires reassurance that there is immediate and round-the-clock access to professional services. Obviously, a service provider who is *always* on call stands a far better chance of retaining a competitive edge than one who is only sporadically available.

No airline in Europe offers round the clock service. But, if passenger transport could be fully liberalized and one airline then offered round the clock booking - as is the case in the United States - then all the others would be forced to follow suit.

The maintenance sector provides an excellent example of this. Repairs and maintenance have to be available on call: if a specific problem cannot be satisfactorily solved within a specific timeframe, then senior management will cast about for another solution.

Group 4 Securitas, for example, is always on call - and not only when there is an immediate threat to security. Similarly, S.W.I.F.T. software engineers are on permanent standby at weekends, irrespective of the fact that the system is remarkably trouble-free.

Applying a just-in-time approach to services is a recipe for disaster. It is a guarantee that the competition will be ready to step in-and take over. Forcing your own organization to be able to respond to an "all-the time" marketing approach may very well be the key to success. Ask yourself this: is a database *really* a database if it is not permanently accessible?

The best example of permanent availability probably comes from the temporary personnel market. Temporary employment agencies have built their success on the simple fact that qualified personnel - workmen, technicians, secretaries, receptionists, or even managers - are available 100% of the time. In effect, without this all-the-time approach, the *raison d'être* of such firms as Manpower, ECCO or Adia would not exist.

Key Success Factors

Success in manufacturing industry is a function of access to raw materials, cheap capital, a competent workforce and technology. By contrast, services have no raw material requirements, and their organizational technologies cannot be patented. Clearly, success in services must depend on other factors. As we have already suggested, the central precondition is the workforce. Services are personal, manufacturing is impersonal.

Today, when manufacturing industry is laying off workers left, right and centre, the services sector is looking desperately for qualified personnel. In fact, not the acquisition but the retention of qualified personnel (37) is one of the most important challenges to the services sector.

A services business is infinitely more dependent on the quality of its personnel than its manufacturing counterparts. What is more, in manufacturing there is a clearly discernible trend towards substituting people by means of automation and industrial robotics. It is only in exceptional cases that this type of substitution is feasible and practical in the services context.

To put it bluntly, it is not a question of attracting staff: *keeping* your best staff is the principal challenge facing services management.

A first priority in this respect is the creation of a viable corporate culture.

Incontestably, a service organization is under substantially more pressure than a manufacturing group to reflect and project the lifestyle aspirations of its staff. In manufacturing, the emphasis quickly shifts to wage negotiations, working hours and vacation entitlements. But, in a fast-growing services organization, it is all too evident that higher wages can quickly be offset by substantially increased fiscal pressures. It is not simply by paying them more that you can keep the best staff.

It is for this reason that services companies frequently offer a wide range of lifestyle services (49). These might include, for example, a *crèche* or kindergarten facility, which will enable working mothers to return to work earlier, secure in the knowledge that the baby is well taken care of nearby and free from the pressures of having to dash off at five-thirty or six to pick up the baby. How many mothers would not like to be able to feed their baby over lunch or give it a cuddle during a coffee-break? When S.W.I.F.T. introduced this service, and received widespread publicity for it, hundreds of expecting mothers, highly qualified and with a wealth of experience, wrote indicating they would like to consider working for S.W.I.F.T..

Other firms offer car maintenance facilities: cars break down, as we all know only too well, and they also need to be washed and polished. Offering this in-house is a valued incentive. Some firms have instituted a shopping facility: you come into the office in the morning, hand in your shopping list to the reception or the security guard and, at the close of the business day, find your groceries already in the trunk of your car. Another useful facility is a direct line to the office installed at home, so that working mothers can function when the children are on holiday or when someone in the household is ill.

Lifestyle services such as these are proving more attractive to key workers than more traditional incentives like a marginally higher income or a longer paid vacation. Although some of these facilities may appear to be unnecessary extras today, they will in future become standard features of services sector employment, not to mention a vital consideration in attracting and retaining top-flight staff.

There are no schools which teach telemarketing, and database consultancy is not, to our knowledge, a common subject on today's curricula. As a result, many service industries opt for staff who have a *prima facie* attitude that suggests they will adapt to these functions and enjoy working in them.

Of course, once they have acquired the necessary skills, it would be stupid to risk losing them. As a result, it is becoming increasingly common for contracts of employment to be highly flexible. What the European Commission not so long ago labelled "atypical" (38) is becoming progressively "typical".

In effect, many employees may wish to work 2,000 hours per year and the company may very well have to agree to a flexible pattern of employment distribution over the year. The nine-to-five job is not only inefficient from the viewpoint of the marketplace, which requires an all-the-time availability, it is also unacceptable to many who resent the "subway-job-subway-bed" syndrome: this is *not* what qualified staff in services companies are signing up for...

These comments should not be taken to suggest that a company only has to take care of the employees wishes in term of lifestyle and training. On the contary, an appropriate financial award system is indeed most welcome, even necessary in order to forge a shift from the product strategy approach to a real client strategy. But, it is unacceptable to claim that the company has evolved into a client strategy company when the financial rewards for the staff are still sales-based.

Any extra financial reward scheme should be based on the results obtained by the client (41). This is perhaps new, but not so difficult, on the condition that the company undertakes an audit of the expectations of the client and the result for the client. These elements should offer the necessary parameters to detemine a result based reward system. If, on the other hand, no such audit has been undertaken, then indeed, we have the tendency to focus only on sales results, the upshot being that the company remains product-oriented and not driven by the objectives and solutions to which its clients aspire.

Marketing

The recent trend towards contracting out professional services to specialized groups that know their subsector inside out has its roots in simple acceptance of the fact that these are most likely better-placed to evaluate a client's needs than the client himself.

When a manufacturing plant contracts out security services or maintenance, or software, it is typically because the client himself does not have a clearly-defined concept of his own needs. In other words, there is not only the need to know the business, creativity is as much an ingredient as experience and intelligence.

In essence, the provider of business support services is supplying input to the client strategy (11) rather than selling products and services neatly laid-out in a catalogue. A manufacturing firm has a range of products that it develops in line with technological know-how and conditions of market demand and competitive forces. The services group that targets this market *must* monitor the client's strategy. As a result, management differs significantly between manufacturing and services.

When a salesman visits a customer, he is usually said to be making a "sales call". The objective is clear cut: he is trying to make a sale. The situation is totally different in a services context. A meeting with the client very quickly takes on all the salient features of a strategy session (12). Processing the information that becomes available during such a session when views are openly exchanged quickly develops into an atmosphere of trust which enables strategic data to be exchanged.

A smoothly-functioning communications system is a *sine qua non* if the service provider is to be ready to act and react swiftly to the client's needs (whether or not these are clearly expressed by the client himself). The best services company will position itself as a counsel to the client and preempt key decisions.

In order to be able to respond to the variety of needs, the service provider has to have a good understanding of the dynamics of the business his client is in. How many information technology manufacturers have segmented their markets according to the businesses which invest most in computer and telecom systems? Few, if any. All segmentation of the market is based on traditional economic sub-divisions: textiles, steel, chemicals, financial services, government ... forgetting that these are all near to zero-growth industries where only replacement orders can be expected (although these are clearly important as well).

In fact, not one IT company has systematically approached the 50 double-digit growth services on the European market which are in urgent need of solutions tailored to their needs and means. But, with investments in information systems well above 1% of turnover, these are the markets to target. IT specialists will have to employ a series of sector analysts in an effort to understand better what is happening on the market. Just like stockbrokers had to acquire sector-specific expertise each time a new company from an undocumented sector wished to be listed on the stock exchange, so computer manufacturers and other suppliers of goods and services will be forced to accumulate first hand insight on cost structure, market development and key success factors for each of these fast-growing businesses.

In an industrial environment, it is assumed that the manufacturer has thoroughly analyzed the changing market situation and that, in contract negotiations with his customers, has successfully complied as far as possible with product specifications (13). However, if S.W.I.F.T., for example, had allowed its participating financial institutions to determine the form and format of its standard interbank messages, discussions would still be going on to this day. In fact, it was S.W.I.F.T., working in conjunction with its constituent member institutions, that determined the appropriate configuration of interbank messages to be carried over its networks. And it was S.W.I.F.T. that determined which hardware and which software were needed and imposed these specifications on the computer and telecommunications systems manufacturers.

Similarly, when Federal Express discovered that its clients not only required fast expedition of their documents but also reassurance that the consignments were in secure hands and would be delivered on time, the company immediately set about developing its acclaimed "supertracker" system. Note that Fedex's clients did not specify such a process, but they immediately recognized its value. As a result, of course, other competitors were obliged to follow suit. And as is known by now, none of the IT producers showed interest in designing this solution, considering the market of express courier services too marginal and their own product range too superior to have to adapt to such a small niche.

Profits in the future will certainly depend on the identification and the successful penetration of 1,000 small niches. Who would not like to be recognized as the supplier of solutions to the courier service companies? Who is preparing to offer the solutions needed in telemarketing, three-dimensional video imaging and other areas?

Client Share vs. Market Share

Professional business support services is a market segment that accounts for 6% or so of Europe's gross domestic product and which is growing at an average rate of 15% year-on-year.

This fast expansion means that services is the most future-oriented sector of the European economy. The entry threshold is low and, provided that a firm is properly motivated and properly motivates its people, develops a strong organizational technology, and makes intelligent use of information technology and telecommunications, success is almost guaranteed.

To the extent that market access is relatively simple, the key to double-digit success lies essentially in developing an optimal marketing strategy.

"Business-to-business" is clearly the best form of communication (34) for business support services. This is a marketing technique which the manufacturing sector is only now beginning to accept, however, and - as yet - it is still too often characterized by the type of institutional advertising designed to appeal to potential target groups.

Successful service companies usually have a low institutional profile (36). When you walk past the headquarters of SGS in Geneva or Adia in Lausanne, it is hard to accept that both those companies are in the ECU one billion-plus annual turnover bracket. As it happens, the vast majority of the 75 European service companies with annual turnovers in excess of ECU one billion are very low-profile indeed.

They are as low-profile as their manufacturing counterparts are high-profile. There are obvious exceptions to this rule, but they only serve to confirm it: Maxwell and Berlusconi may be headline-grabbers, but it is Bertelsmann which is number one in the publishing world. Bertelsmann is based in Gütersloh, Germany. Ever been there?

It is not only in communications strategies that the services sector exhibits different parameters from its manufacturing counterpart.

Manufacturing industries talk market share to evidence their success and power. Granted, the Japanese have taught us an interesting lesson in postulating market share as a strategic success factor and alternative to outright profits and return on investment. But market share obscures the number of clients lost due to bad management, and balances it all with quick marketing and volume sales.

In the new services, there is another parameter: instead of simply looking at market share, successful service companies use *client share* (10) as a key indicator of lasting success in the marketplace.

Why?

Quite simply because, first of all, the cost of acquiring a *new* client is some four times greater than the cost of increasing turnover at the level of an existing client. Every customer, every plant that buys in services or opts to use a particular firm's services, is potentially a user of *more* services from that selfsame source. Ultimately, the service provider will be performing not one service but a *cluster* of services, a range of individual services that are closely related one to the next and that can be offered to the customer in a coordinated way. This is the basis for economies of scope (19): how to do *more* business with your largest clients.

For example, consider the case of a market leader in language services, INK. What this implies is that INK does not only provide translations. Far from it. The company boasts a sophisticated computerized network, which directly delivers computer diskettes to the client, which can provide artwork and layout facilities, and much, much more besides. Today's leading language management groups are positioned to offer electronic publishing facilities, not to mention software conversion. Which services sector is the translation company in? Translation? Publishing? Computers? Graphics? Software? And what about the software company? Is it in custom designed software, consulting, facilities management, training, education, or systems integration?

As was indicated at the beginning of this book, there is an erosion of the boundaries between sectors (4) and this makes it extremely difficult to determine what market share you actually control. It is nearly impossible to undertake a sound competitive analysis (8) because the latest and strongest competition may be coming from a corner you never expected it from in the first place.

To put it in a nutshell: it is often infinitely preferable to ignore macro-sectoral projections and simply concentrate on providing clients with as comprehensive a service as possible. In the case of the language management company INK, translation services may provide the point of entry but, properly managed, this will be no more than a first stepping-stone towards provision of a whole gamut of specialized services offered singly or in conjunction with other specialty groups. This is how a strategic interest in the client's business is gradually built up. And, if you cannot offer the service the client has asked for, you can always network (22) with the one that is capable of supplying under your umbrella. Service companies do not have the same urge to acquire each other. Some who have tried have paid for it dearly as the Blue Arrow and Saatchi & Saatchi cases have demonstrated all too vividly.

Admittedly, it is difficult to determine one's exact market share or quantify one's competitive position. That is one more reason not to use market share as a key determinant of success. Achieving a higher client share will immediately impact favourably on the bottom line and give the means to monitor the evolution of the strategic relationship with the best clients. And, ultimately, this results in a higher market share - not only in one but in several sectors.

Services companies should not ignore market share - quite the contrary. But to build market share, the immediate short-term objective must be to develop client share. This is perhaps one of the best kept secrets of Japan. The industry in the Land of the Rising Sun monitors client share on a weekly and monthly basis. In other words, they do have very well defined - short term - objectives, but admit improving client shares each month is of greater importance to the long-term success of the company than earnings per share per quarter.

When will *you* start applying client share strategy?

Epilogue

There are no surefire blueprints for success, no cast-iron guarantees of double-digit growth. What is more, it would be presumptuous to pretend that there are. That said, let's close with three truncated checklists - one for politicians gearing up for the next election campaign, one for policymakers in charge of charting the economy of tomorrow and one for services company executives with both feet on the ground.

Ten reasons why POLITICIANS up for reelection should pay closer attention to services

1. Services make manufacturing more competitive
2. Services are environment-friendly
3. Services represent growth
4. Services generate more jobs than any other sector
5. Services respond to local needs
6. **New** services do not require subsidies
7. Services companies spend more on training than companies in any other sector
8. Services companies exhibit a minimal lead time between decision and implementation
9. Services are highly-diversified, thus less vulnerable in periods of economic downturn; and
10. Services offer opportunities both to local entrepreneurs **and** international investors.

Ten issues POLICYMAKERS should address when charting the future course of their country or region

1. What are the potential local comparative advantages for services of the region?

2. Which services are locally consumed but supplied from elsewhere?

3. Which services could respond to local demand and generate jobs tailored to the qualifications (or lack of qualifications) of job seekers?

4. How can an economically adversely-affected region develop services? Specifically, what kind of infrastructure based on information technology, telecommunications, marketing, training and lifestyle facilities must be put in place to stimulate future oriented services?

5. Which services are in full swing internationally but not yet available locally?

6. How can manufacturing industry become more competitive via twinning with new services?

7. How can developing countries identify and develop new services to compete more effectively and generate higher value-added in agro-produce?

8. Which type of trade promotion can the government undertake to support the export of services in which the country or region has a clear competitive advantage?

9. How can employer/employee relationships be restructured on the basis of these new factors in the job market?

10. Which research and development policies should the government pursue to support the growth of services?

Ten Golden Rules for the Services Company Executive

1. Spread two categories of contagious diseases throughout your company: enthusiasm and smiles

2. **Never** cut first of all the training budget

3. Think hard and aloud about how to make innovative use of available technologies

4. When a good idea surfaces, do something with it - don't just talk about it

5. **Never** settle for anything less than the quality expected by your clients. Settle for more.

6. Explore how you can keep your colleagues happy without handing too much money to the taxman

7. If you are short of cash, invite your best client to become a shareholder (18)

8. Don't become obsessive about your core business: think and act in clusters of services, perhaps using the European Economic Interest Grouping approach

9. Never miss a chance to explain to the politicians how you make things happen in services and how your cost structure differs from manufacturing,

10. Support your labour union representatives to help them explain to their superiors how services companies train, inform and consult their employees as an integral part of building a competitive company capable of maintaining double-digit growth.

For further information, feel free to contact the author at:

't Hooghuys
B-2590 Berlaar
Belgium

Tel: 32 (3) 482.47.91
Fax: 32 (3) 482 47 96

COMPARISON MAN~

SERVICES   ## INDUSTRY

MARKET CHARACTERISTICS

	SERVICES	INDUSTRY
1.	Double-digit growth	Slow growth
2.	People, C&C, life style services	Capital, raw materials technologies & people
3.	Low barriers to entry	High barriers to entry
4.	Erosion of the boundaries	Core business strategy
5.	Low level of government intervention	High level of government intervention
6.	No market data	Broadly documented

COMPETITION

7.	Collaborate & compete	Secrecy
8.	Broad competitive analyses	Narrow competitive analysis

CLIENT RELATION

9.	Personnel first	Client is the king
10.	Clients' share	Market share
11.	Client strategy	Product strategy
12.	Strategy meetings	Sales calls
13.	Determine standards with the client	Come as close as possible to specs

TIME

14.	Be there when needs arise	Monitor changes on the market
15.	After-purchase challenge	Pre-purchase challenge
16.	All the time	Just in time

GROWTH AND BOTTOM LINE STRATEGY

17.	Investment in time	Cash injection
18.	First client first shareholder	Third party financing
19.	Economics of scope	Economies of scale
20.	Personnel management most important	Marketing most important
21.	Multi-disciplinary approach	Specialist approach
22.	Networking	Acquisition strategy
23.	Built-in obsolesence	Long product life cycle
24.	Decentralized	Centralized
25.	Purchasing is the process	Production process
26.	Cost of result	Cost of production

SERVICES	**INDUSTRY**

QUALITY

27. Quality control is self-control	Third party quality control
28. Quality is the multiplication	Quality is the sum
29. Quality most valued by clients	Price most valued by clients
30. Service liability not insurable	Product liability can be insured

TECHNOLOGY

31. Organisational technologies	Product- and process technologies
32. Use of technologies	Development of technologies
33. Service infrastructure	Industrial infrastructure

MARKETING

34. Business to business marketing	Advertising
35. Non-existence of HQ	Prestigious HQ
36. Discrete	Visible

HUMAN RESOURCES

37. Keep personnel	Recruit and train personnel
38. A-typical work contracts	Typical work contracts
39. The capacity to fail	Punish failures and successes
40. Loose hierarchy	Strict hierarchy
41. Result based reward	Sales based reward
42. Fast changing career path	Predictable career path

PERSONNEL QUALIFICATIONS

43. Attitude based recruitment	Education & experience based recruitment
44. Communication skills	Production skills
45. Talk the language of the client	Talk the language of your boss
46. Personnel speaks three languages	Personnel speaks English
47. Always responsible	Only responsible for your area
48. Define your own training needs	Personnel dep. defines needs
49. Motivated by life style	Motivated by money
50. Eye for detail	Eye for quantity

EUROPEAN COMPANIES LEAD	***EUROPEAN COMPANIES FOLLOW***

© G. Pauli 1990

Services studied in this book

Traditional Services

financial services
  banking
  retail financial services
  wholesale banking
  investment banking
  stock dealing
  venture capital
insurance
  reinsurance
  life-insurance
  non-life insurance
accountancy and audit
engineering services
trade and distribution services
  barter trade
  import/export houses

New and Innovative services
1. MARKETING SERVICES

marketing services
  public relations
  market research / fax polls
  advertising services
direct marketing services
  telemarketing
trade fairs and exhibitions
  international conferences
  meeting management services
  incentive conferencing
  press conference organization
  product presentation
  hostess services
design services
  interior design
  industrial design
  architectural concept development
  automobile prototype product design
  and development

design consultancy
corporate identity design
three-dimensional video imaging
graphic design
CAD/CAM services
brochure / annual services design
package design
media services
  media monitoring and research
  electronic media services
  cable television services
  satellite telecom services

2. PERSONNEL RELATED SERVICES

human resource management
  personnel management
  career development services
  outplacement
  executive search
  personnel selection and recruitement
  consulting
  temporary executives placement
  training organizing and consultancy
language courses
distance education
public speaking
management motivation training
computer courses and training (hardware
/software)
professional moving services
  door-to-door transportation
  domestic relocation
  warehouse services
  international removals
  document archiving and preservation
  services
  document supply services

3. COMPUTER AND TELECOM

software services
- custom designed software
- entertainment software
- software engineering
- transport software services
- packaged software
- debugging
- language programming

computer services
- electronic publishing
- electronic mail
- electronic distribution
- system intregration
- integrated communication system design

telecommunication
- datacasting
- line leasing
- telex network
- fax polling
- VAN, LAN
- HIMS
- interbank communication
- interactive data communication

4. LIFE STYLE SERVICES

teleservices
- teleshopping
- telemaintenance
- teleauctioning
- telebanking
- teleconferencing
- telebetting
- telecontrol services
- teleprinting
- teleguarding
- interactive financial telecommunication

convenience services
- mail order
- catalogue shopping
- shoe repair
- cutlery sharpening
- key duplication
- photo development
- watch repair
- clothing repair
- personalized printing

travel related services
- business travel
- tourist services
- tour operating

medical services
- hospital management
- health care services
- computerized medical data services

leisure services
- amusement and theme park services

cultural services
- theatre ticketing
- artwork services
- art gallery
- student exchanges
- other lifestyle services
- car care
- kindergarten
- plastic card services
- fitness and sports centres

5. SUPPORT SERVICES

fleet management
- car leasing
- car rental
- car care

courier express services
- courier services
- remailing
- parcel mailing
- express forwarding
- document handling

cleaning and maintenance services
- computer maintenance

contract cleaning services

laundry services
- building maintenance
- hospital maintenance
- dust-free room

linguistic services
- language databanks
- translating services
- conference interpreting
- machine translating
- simultaneous interpretating
- language simplication

quality control and inspection services
- certification
- pre- and postshipment inspection
- statutory inspection
- calibration
- laboratory analysis / testing
- quality assurance / quality control
- metrology laboratory services
- damage survey services
- environmental analysis: air, water, ground, pollution control
- arbitration services
- safety audit services

security services
- manned guarding
- transport of valuables
- electronic security and alarm services
- intruder alarm system services
- data security equipment and services
- access control system services
- teleguarding
- security archiving
- electronic alarm system services
- HIMS
- electronic security services

diverse business support services
- construction engineering
- licensing and patent services
- high quality fax
- telex networking

facilities management
logistical services
legal services
agronomic counselling
environmental services
- refuse collection
- waste management
- environmental consultancy

inventory management
intelligent-building management
information management
consulting /tax advice
social law and social secretariat services
crisis management services
management audit
export advice
marketing services
insolvency analysis and consultancy
temporary employment services
real estate and property management
catering
business information services

publishing
- desk top publishing
- electronic publishing

databank services
- financial and economic information databanks
- industrial database
- patent and trade mark databank services
- scientific databank services
- on-line databank service
- technological and technical information databanks
- electronic financial services
- text retrieval services
- CD Rom and datastorage services
- information brokering

INDEX

Other books by the same author

The Crusader for the Future: a biography of Aurelio Peccei, founder of the Club of Rome. 1987, published by Pergamon Press

Services: the driving force of the economy. 1987, published by Waterlow Publications.
(also available in French, Dutch and Norwegian)

The Second Wave: Japan's global assault on financial services. co-authored with Prof. Dr. Richard Wright. 1987, published by Waterlow Publications (UK) and Saint Martin's Press (US).
(also available in French, Italian, German, Japanese, Portuguese)

Doen! autobiographic notes. 1989, published by Roularta Books. Only available in Dutch.

Double Digit Growth: How to Achieve It with Services. 1991 is also available in Dutch, French, Spanish, German.

Order Form

company/organisation: _____

title mrs/mr/ms/dr/ir/prof: _____

first name: _____ surname: _____

position: _____

street and n°: _____

city: _____ zip code: _____

country: _____

tel: _____ telefax: _____

orders _____ copies of "Double-Digit Growth" in
orders _____ copies of "Second Wave: Japan's Assault on
              Financial Services" in
orders _____ copies of "Services: the driving force of the economy" in

O English   O French   O Dutch

at the price of 695 Belgian francs each, VAT and delivery included

would like to receive the latest Annual Report of the following
ESIF member companies

O Telinfo   O Group 4 Securitas
O DHL   O ATENCO
O ATI Travel   O S.W.I.F.T.
O TMI   O Roularta
O Thilly Van Eessel   O ADIA
O GREGG Interim   O SGS
O ISS   O BET
O Arthur Pierre   O KPMG
O ESIF   O Control y Aplicaciones

Return to ESIF, 't Hooghuys, B-2590 Berlaar, Belgium

NOTES